OCCASIONAL ESSAYS ON NATIVE SOUTH INDIAN LIFE

OCCASIONAL ESSAYS
ON
NATIVE SOUTH INDIAN LIFE

STANLEY P. RICE

GYAN

Published by

Gyan Publishing House
5, Ansari Road
Daryaganj, New Delhi-110002
Phone: 011-47034999, 9811692060
E-mail: books@gyanbooks.com

Distribution Network
gyanbooks.com
India, USA, Canada, UK, Australia, France

ISBN : 978-81-212-3839-7 (PB)
First Published, London, 1901

2nd Impression 2020

Printed at: Gyan Press, Delhi.

Occasional Essays on Native South Indian Life
Author: Stanley P. Rice

OCCASIONAL ESSAYS

ON

NATIVE SOUTH INDIAN LIFE

BY

STANLEY P. RICE

INDIAN CIVIL SERVICE

LONGMANS, GREEN, AND CO.

39 PATERNOSTER ROW, LONDON

NEW YORK AND BOMBAY

1901

PREFACE

De Quincey somewhere says that, if he stopped to consider what is proper to be said, he would soon come to doubt whether any part at all is proper. In writing the following pages I have stopped to consider, and the inevitable misgiving has often caused me to lay down my pen. Much that I have written must, it seemed to me, be already well known, and what was new was probably not worth knowing. Hoping, however, that peradventure there may be some men to whom these papers will be interesting, I have taken courage to submit them to the public.

Amongst the many books which have been published on India and Indian topics, it is rare to find one that treats of the South. Since the time of Clive and Hyder Ali, historical interest has centred in the North. Travellers prefer to visit the famous cities of the Punjab and the North-West Provinces, the gardens of Kashmir, and the mountains of Nepal, rather than the less attractive towns and districts of the Southern Presidency. There are many reasons why this should be so; and I feel that an apology is almost needed for venturing upon a South Indian topic.

In writing on such subjects, it is almost impossible to avoid the use of some Indian words for which there are no exact English equivalents. In these cases I have added a footnote for the benefit of readers who may not be sufficiently acquainted with India to understand them. It may often happen, too, that what is commonplace to the Anglo-Indian is unintelligible to the English reader, and the task of steering a middle course was not always easy.

My thanks are due to many friends, both English and Indian, who have assisted me with advice and information. I am also indebted to the editor of the *Madras Mail*, who has kindly allowed me to use material contributed to that paper, and to the editor of the *Calcutta Review*, for permission to reprint the paper called "A Forgotten Rebellion."

S. P. R.

CONTENTS

AMONG THE URIYAS

I.

LANGUAGE.

THE task which I have proposed to myself is to set down in my leisure hours a few observations and deductions which, during a stay, short indeed absolutely, but long when compared with the sojourn of most Government officers, I have been able to make concerning manners and customs peculiar to the Uriyas of Ganjam. I do not pretend to have exhausted my subject; I do not pretend to treat it scientifically. Some of my incidents may be commonplace; some customs which I imagine to be peculiar to the district may be mere variations of Southern customs. I claim only this merit, that everything which is set down here, I have either seen myself or have been told by the people, generally in their own language. I give the following pages for what they are worth; but if I shall have only succeeded in stirring up pleasant memories in the minds of those who know the district, I shall not feel that my labour has been in vain.

I imagine that Macaulay's school-boy, who knew "who imprisoned Montezuma and who strangled Atahuallpa," but who could not tell where Sujah Dowlah reigned, is a fit analogy for many nowadays, who have a very hazy idea of the position of Orissa on the map; who could not put their finger on the great seat of the worship of Jagannath; who do not know that Orissa has a special language of its own, spoken by millions, or, if they do know it, have not the remotest idea whether it has greater affinities for Hindi or for Fijian.

And yet the people of Orissa are a distinct race—distinct from the Bengalis to the north and from the Telugu to the south—distinct in features, in manners, in customs, in language especially. Orissa proper lies within the province of Bengal, and the people of Ganjam suffer in that they have been separated from their brethren; they are foundling children, alien from the more favoured, because better recognized Dravidian races; alien even in the origin to which their ancestry has been traced.

The Uriya language is rough and solid, resembling, if I may venture on a somewhat too fanciful simile, the unhewn temples of Salisbury Plain rather than the graceful cathedral of Salisbury city. Indeed, this simile is true in more senses than the obvious one. For as Stonehenge is evidently the work of rude and uncivilized hands, while the cathedral is the production of more cunning artificers, so does Uriya appear, in relation to other languages, as the language of an uncivilized people. The foundation of it is Sanskrit; into the building there have been introduced blocks from Hindustani quarries, and less massive stones from the land of the Telugus; but the old structure remains all the same. It will, I think, be conceded that the progress of a language is away from inflection and synthesis. The two most highly civilized nations in the world—the French and English—use languages which, except in the case of verbs, are almost entirely analytical. Uriya is a highly inflected language. The nouns have separate inflections, denoting possession, place, instrument. The verbs are made to express condition, time, causation, by means of inflection. But I am transgressing my limits. I have no desire to write a treatise on grammar or a philological essay. I shall leave it to my readers to judge of my accuracy when I say that the Uriya for 'at the houses' is "ghorománongkotháré!"

The written character bears a very close

resemblance to the Nagari letters. It has lost the distinguishing line at the top, however, and the angles have all been rounded into curves. I shall be able to convey some idea of what I mean by citing in analogy the relation between the Roman and the German characters; but in the present instance the dissimilarity is far more marked.

There are very few—I may say, none—in Ganjam who can write the language in a cursive hand; almost all the documents that one sees are written in the printed character. So true is it that the people of these parts cannot read or write a cursive hand, that should a document so written be received from beyond the frontier, it is extremely difficult to find any one who can decipher it.

The language may be described as a blend of Sanskrit and Hindustani; I do not, however, use this expression in the strict scientific sense: the basis of the language, especially of the written language, is Sanskrit, but it is not altogether impossible for a man who knows only Hindustani to catch the drift of an Uriya conversation. How far Hindustani has had a direct influence on the language, and how far both languages have borrowed similar words and similar structures from the Sanskrit it is not the province of this essay to discuss. One curious fact is worth recording; it is that the vowel-sound which in many Oriental languages is *understood* (though not written) with consonants, and which in other Indian languages is represented by a short "a" becomes in Uriya a primitive "o" sound.

One of the characteristics which betrays that the Uriya language has not progressed, and that the nation is still in the infancy of its civilization, is the fondness for onomatopoetic words. It is natural that tribes in a primitive state, who wished to express some object in speech, should coin words suggested by some sound made by the object, whether it be a living being or a natural phenomenon. "Kukkuda" is the word for a fowl, and it is a clear imitation of the call which has led us to christen the bird "Cock-a-doodle-doo." "Bromboro" is not a bad reproduction in miniature of the humming of those peculiarly objectionable and stupid beetles which thrust themselves in one's face, often at the most critical moment. Again, "chinkibaro," if you violently accentuate the first syllable, tells its own tale; no interpreter is needed to inform us that this is the word for "to sneeze."

The Sanskrit element appears very prominently

in Uriya names. As far as my experience of Telugu names has gone, I have found that the lower classes use purely vernacular names, not to be traced to any Sanskrit form, and not representing either the gods of the true Hindu mythology or their attributes. Even among the educated classes the names are confined to variations of a root form; variations, for instance, on the root form Jagat, variations on the names Rama, Krishna, Sita. The only name I can at present remember which conveys any picture to the mind is the name Narasimham, the man-lion; but as that is an incarnation, and not an attribute, of Vishnu, it is hardly a case in point.

Amongst the Uriyas, however, the appellations derived from the attributes of the gods are many and various. Syamo-sundara means "of a beautiful bluish colour," and is an attribute of Krishna. Krishna, too, is the "Dhonu-dhara" or bow-bearer, the far-darting Apollo of Hindu lore. Brundavano means a forest of the sacred "tulasi" plant. We may hope that he who bears the name "Nityananda" (always rejoicing) is as free from care as his name suggests. "Dásarathi" is a good instance of the purely Sanskrit character of these names. It is derived from Dasaratha (ten cars) by pure Sanskrit derivative method. I do not wish to multiply instances, though I find many more ready to my hand. Just as in Homer we find the "constant epithet," so that Athéné is "γλαυκῶπις, Heré is λευκώλενος, Apollo is ἑκάεργος; so the Uriya people have seized on the epithets, and call their sons "grey-eyed" and "far-darting," while their Telugu neighbours have rather adopted the names themselves of the gods.

In default of a better name Robinson Crusoe called the savage whose life he saved "Friday," that being the day of their meeting. The lower classes of the Uriya people have a custom from which Defoe has unconsciously borrowed. The names Sombaria (Monday), Sukria (Friday), are not at all uncommon, and Sunday and Thursday have also been requisitioned. Why Saturday should not be used is not inexplicable, for from the time of the earliest Accadian mythology Saturday has been a day of evil omen; and many a Hindu has as superstitious a dread of beginning an undertaking on Saturday as some amongst us have of going on a journey on Friday, or of sitting down thirteen to table.

The names of which I have been treating are what I may call the Christian names. Generally speaking, the Uriyas have two names—that which serves to distinguish the individual and that which serves to show his caste or sect. Brahmins have many titles, most of which denote in some form or other the overlordship of the ruling class. The highest sect is called "Satopasti," a corruption of satopati, from "swoto" (100) and "pati" (a lord). These are supposed to be the flower of the Brahmin tribe, who receive the homage even of inferior Brahmins. "Panigrahi" is a curious title with a curious history. It appears that when the rajas went a-walking it was not meet for them to walk alone. Certain Brahmins therefore accompanied them—one walking on each side. The raja would place his hands upon the outspread palms of these courtiers, and thus walk along in stately if uncomfortable dignity. From this practice arose the name "Panigrahi"—"he that holdeth the hands."

Those that attend the car, carry the idol, and perform other acts of devotion around the god at Purushottam or Puri, are called Ponda. The derivation of this word is not clear to me, but I believe the word is connected with the root "padh," "to read." This derivation appears more obviously in the name Padhi, the title of another sect of Brahmins, whose duty it is to expound the Védas.

The heads of the village are called "Korono," "the doer," and "Karji," "the manager." Both words are derived from the same root, "kar," though the latter is more directly connected with the word "karjyo," "an affair." It is surely a practical view of life that the Uriya takes, when the village heads are thus the representatives of action. Or perhaps —and this is the more probable view—the village heads are the "doer" and the "manager" *par excellence*, to whom the ryot entrusts all his doing and managing, the better to gratify his own laziness.

The korono, who is really only the accountant, but who, by reason of his higher education, is generally the ultimate authority in the village, appropriates to himself as his caste distinction the title "Potonaiko." The word signifies the naik or head of the town. It is curious to find that the word "naiko," which is corrupted into the Telugu "naidu," is the caste distinction of the lowest class, the village watcher and professional thief!

This man, for all that his cognomen is thus lofty, goes by the generic name of "Dandassi." This word means "worthy of punishment;" and assuredly no appellation ever fitted its owner more completely than does this. He is the village policeman and the village thief—a curious mixture of callings! The villagers seem to have acted on the proverb, "Set a thief to catch a thief;" and if they do not always manage to catch their thief, they at least live up to their maxim in setting one!

Before quitting the subject of men's names—and I fear lest I grow tedious—I must mention one which I think is worthy of explanation. The word for a barber is "Bhondari." This word is derived from "bhondaram," a treasure. Not much connection, one would think, between treasure and a barber, unless it be that with razor, ruthless as the shears of Atropos, he sometimes shaves the precious moustache, or demolishes the delicately nurtured whisker. The real truth is that the zemindars * delivered over the guarding of the treasure to the professional barber, who became a more important person in this capacity than in his original office of "shaver in ordinary to his Highness." The name has survived; the office has given place to one which the average reader will consider more of a necessity and less of a luxury.

* A zemindar is a landed proprietor, who generally keeps up on a small scale the state of a raja. His estate is called a "zemindari."

But while most Uriyas have only two names, many are to be met with in the zemindaris who boast of three or even four. The additions are for the most part titles given by the various zemindars, and they are often even more easily acquired than some knighthoods and many medals! A title, generally accompanied by more substantial recognition, in the shape of land, is given for "blessing" the zemindar, for holding his umbrella, perhaps for handing him betel leaves. Sir Walter Raleigh is not the only one whose entrance into Court favour was carpeted with a muddy cloak of plush!

Thus titles for the most part denote some sort of compliment, such as "Bhushano," an ornament, "Ratno," a jewel, or "Subuddhi," the wise. Others, again, seem to have no meaning, but are simply fanciful names invented by the zemindars.

"What's in a name?" cried the passionate Juliet; and she was right, for to her Romeo was Romeo, though he were christened Tom or Dick. But we who live in a later and more dispassionate age, who are wont to look at things in the full light of practical common-sense, or in the cold, dry light of scientific research, may be allowed to ascribe some virtue to a name.

Names are not given to men or to towns as numbers are to convicts and American streets. There was a reason, probably, for every name—an æsthetic reason, perhaps, but still a reason. No more direct instances can be found than those which occur in the Bible. The Israelites, even in the course of their march across the desert, named the places from fortuitous circumstances. Marah, bitterness, and Meribah, strife, testify to the accidents to which the names are due. Nor is it incident alone which suggests names. Jericho, the city of palm trees, Bethphage, and Bethany, betray in their names the natural features of the places which they distinguish.

The history of a place and the character of its people are often bound up in its name. Thus, in our own England, the affix "chester" shows the Roman occupation, "ton" is West Saxon, while "by" indicates a settlement of the Danes ; and is there not a whole volume of history in this ?

If the Uriyas show peculiarities in the names they choose for their children, the names of their villages must also be allowed to be in many cases imaginative. Unfortunately, many of the low country villages are called by names which are so corrupted that it is very difficult to trace their meaning now. There are, however, one or two instances which will serve to illustrate this remark. "Nolihaddo," the hollow bone, suggests grim legends, but "Gangadohoni," the Uriya name for the flower called "gloriosa superba," calls up visions of sweet lanes and scented hedgerows, of an Indian "bank whereon the wild thyme grows." Alas! poor vision! rudely dissipated by the stern reality of cowsheds and the common native huts of mud and thatch. Nothing could resemble less an English country lane; nothing could remind one less of the brilliant scarlet and yellow of the flower whose name the village bears.

In the mountains, where Nature made a more direct impression on the Uriya mind, there are many fanciful and imaginative names. An Oriental poet has told us that "the high hills are a refuge for the wild goats." From the plains below the Uriya looked up on the steep hills, strewn with rocks and boulders, over which he must climb to his first settlement. It was not surprising, therefore, that he christened the place "Chelligodo," or the Fortress of the Goat. In the next halting-place was a high hill, and the Uriyas going out to their labour in the morning would see the sun rise over this hill day after day. The Hill of Sunrise is not an inappropriate name for the village.

The radiance of the sun and moon seem especially to have struck them, and the glories of the sunset seem to have inspired the name of one village, Subarnagiri, or the Hill of Shining Gold!

It happened that on a dark and stormy night, while the river ran high, a young Mussulman prince was riding a black charger along its banks. Terrified by the howling of the storm and by the vivid flashes of lightning, or perhaps goaded on by the malice of the Evil One, the animal became unmanageable and plunged into the rushing stream. Neither horse nor rider was ever seen again. But the "Ghodo Haddo," the Bones of the Horse, flows over its sandy bed, the grave of the prince and his steed, as it flowed on that stormy night.

In one of those deadly quarrels which sometimes arise between branches of the same house, matters had gone too far for reconciliation. A duel was fought between the brothers; nor had it an end until

> "Side by side those chiefs of pride
> Together fell down dead."

Thus they fought and died, and their memory survives. The place is called Mundomorai, "the Smiting of the Heads."

II.

MANNERS AND CUSTOMS.

It is a tradition amongst those of the Madras Presidency whose fortune has never taken them into the Ganjam district, to conceive of the Uriya as an inferior animal—as belonging to a race not merely low in the rank of civilization, but incapable of better things. As a ryot he is unambitious, as a clerk he is incorrigibly dull, as a man he is far behind the age even of his next-door neighbour, the Telugu. The tradition has become so firmly rooted in the minds of those who have given the subject a thought, that the defects of the Uriya are generally ascribed to something inherent in himself, or to his racial qualities, and very little account is taken of outside influences. The Uriya of Ganjam labours under two disadvantages. He is very far from Madras, and he inhabits only part of a district. He speaks a language which is spoken in Bengal, but not in any part of the Madras Presidency save Ganjam, unless we except the Uriya hill-tribes of Jeypore in the Vizagapatam district; these, however, need scarcely be taken into account. It is rather curious to notice that in a recent Madras Act,* in which are enumerated the various names by which a village headman is known in various districts, the Uriya alone is unrepresented. The fact is significant, for it shows how little he is considered, nay, how entirely his existence is ignored.

But if the Uriya has been under a disadvantage, owing to the paucity of his numbers, and to his want of affinity with the other inhabitants of the Presidency, this disadvantage is as nothing compared with his geographical position. The Uriyas of Ganjam inhabit a long and narrow district in the extreme north of the Presidency, three hundred miles from Calcutta and six hundred from Madras—a district to which till lately access could only be had by sea—whose main port is an open roadstead, always dangerous, and often impracticable. Those who sit in high places, who made it their business to visit southern districts, rarely paid a visit to Ganjam. There was no inducement for the men of other districts to come to him; still less was there any inducement for the Uriya to go south, where his language would be

* The Village Service Cess Act.

unknown, and where all his ambition would be swamped by an overwhelming competition.

The consequence of these disadvantages is that education has languished. The goal of an Uriya boy who wishes to educate himself, is to be master of Telugu—to be acquainted with Uriya. The schoolmaster who is not trained in Madras is generally trained at Rajahmundry on the Godavari. He has probably learnt such Uriya as he possesses from a foreigner. I remember seeing a suggestion made that a professor of Uriya, who really knew the language, should be appointed at Rajahmundry. Even a French boy, whose youth had been given to learning English, and whose knowledge of French literature was simply what he could glean from an English master in an English school, would not make a good instructor, save perhaps to kindergartens. Thus arises a want of qualified Uriya teachers to train those who, in their turn, are to instruct Uriya boys in the various village schools. Too often it happens that the schoolmaster who has set up on his own account has himself only the knowledge which will suffice to take his pupils as far as the rules of money calculation, and the reading of a simple book.

With those ideas which are born of tradition and

fostered by prejudice, it has been the custom to decry the Uriya as a dirty, lazy lout, certainly dissolute, and probably drunken, whose only virtue is an unobtrusiveness, due to his insignificance. The causes of this view of the Uriya are these. In the first place, as I said before, there is a tradition that the Uriya is an inferior animal, and hence arises a desire to prove that tradition correct—by *a posteriori* arguments, if by nothing better. To this end the observer is blind to the virtues, which are not apparent, and notices only the vices, which are. This unconscious desire to make observed facts fit in with a preconceived theory, ignoring those facts which modify, if they do not destroy it, is a failing to which all are prone, and which might of itself account for the present estimation of the Uriya. But there is another cause. It is in just those avocations of life in which the Uriya is thrown into contact with the European, that he fails. Give him a piece of work to do; he is dilatory beyond all bounds of delay. If I were to choose a national motto for him it would be this :—

> "To-morrow, and to-morrow, and to-morrow,
> To the last syllable of recorded time."

Have you broken anything? He will mend it in a

clumsy way. Is the work to be done of a kind requiring skilled labour? He will pass the day in doing a minimum of work and in enjoying a maximum of leisure; wherein, perhaps, according to his philosophy, he is not much to blame.

But his cardinal vice—his besetting sin—is his extreme dirtiness. The ordinary Uriya seems to love being filthy—filthy in his person, filthy in his house, filthy in his surroundings. Go into an Uriya village, and you will find the place stacked with rubbish—filth in the streets, filth on the houses; the whole village looking more like an extended cattle shed than an ordinary habitation of civilized men. The very drinking-water tank is sometimes hardly fit to bathe in.

Here, then, we have a key to the Englishman's opinion of the Uriya. The two gods that sit in the highest places in his national temple are Energy and Cleanliness. To the vicious man who is but energetic and clean, many of his vices are forgiven, but even the virtues of the upright shall not save him from damnation if he worship not these supreme deities. I have said that the Uriya is lazy; I have said he is dirty. The conclusion is obvious. But we must even now be careful not to judge too much by appearances.

Certain customs (to which I shall refer later on), such as the use of saffron and the position of the cowhouse, lend to the person and to the surroundings of the Uriya an appearance of ostentatious dirtiness which the facts do not really justify, and I think I may say, after having seen both, that the interior of an Uriya house is neither better nor worse than that of a Telugu of the same class, unless, perhaps, it is humbler, in that it is of smaller dimensions.

In spite of this, however, have we not realized the picture which was sketched at the beginning? We have found the Uriya infinitely lazy and indescribably dirty, while it has also been indirectly admitted that he is deficient in intelligence. But this is not the whole picture, though these are unfortunately the features which force themselves upon a superficial observer. Let us look a little deeper, and we shall find that the Uriya is for the most part a law-abiding citizen, not complaining and not turbulent, comparatively faithful in his domestic relations, and, above all things, sober. The Uriyas in the hill tracts and at the foot of the hills are, it is true, wilder than their brethren of the sea coast. But they are not a criminal tribe; their turbulence expresses itself in open revolt; they are not the enemies of the human race, as are the cattle lifters and highway robbers of the southern districts. Though, of course, the thieving classes exist, as well as the receivers, without whom the others would soon become extinct, yet ordinarily it may be said that the Uriya does not disturb the safety of the public.

On the other hand, he is quite ready for a fight, and in this respect he is not wanting in *esprit de corps*. I have no desire to write a history of the district, but I may advert to the wars in Gumsur, where the Uriyas rallied round their raja and gave a lot of trouble to the British, although the superior discipline and equipments of the latter made short work of the native resistance; yet in many cases the resistance was offered, and at one place, a village called Alládigám, the English attack was repulsed with considerable loss. A more conspicuous instance of patriotism is to be found in the history of the sale of the Atagada estate. This estate was sold for arrears of revenue in 1854, but the ryots flatly refused to acknowledge any raja but their own. Stringent measures had to be resorted to then, but the same spirit of disaffection has been breaking out ever since. About 20 years ago the diwán of the zemindar of Kallikot (who bought the estate) was murdered by the disaffected ryots. They refused to be sold with the estate to the highest bidder.

The Uriya does not drink, and in this respect he forms a notable contrast to his Telugu brethren. I have seen whole villages of Telugus—of the Reddika caste—in which there was not one man who did not bear the brand of drunkenness on his face. This makes the Telugu turbulent and quarrelsome. A fight in an Uriya village may arise from some sectarian quarrel, or even upon some trivial matter, which serves two embittered factions as a pretext; in a Telugu village a fight will arise for no reason whatever. The Uriya people are often found to be attached even to minute points of religious observance. I was myself at what threatened to be a riot. Two factions adhered to the worship of different gods. Cars were being driven round the village by each, and each strove to force the other into striking the first blow, for the people were on the verge of open war. At last one car overstepped the prescribed boundary by the breadth of one wheel. Instantly the other side attacked it, and I have no doubt would have done damage, had not I been able to restrain their violence. This fanatical spirit is very strong amongst them, and its influence is certainly not for good. The car festival is an annual opportunity for paying off old scores. The followers of Athanasius were not more embittered against the disciples of Arius than are some village factions against one another. Nor are there wanting those who cloak their personal animosities in the ample folds of the garment of religious enthusiasm ; perhaps, indeed, they are the majority, though, looking back on the histories of religions, one might find it hard to say what cannot be done in the name of an adored deity.

Of their domestic relations, since the women are secluded, it is only possible to judge by what comes before the eyes of the world. It is certainly remarkable that the wives who have been deserted by their husbands, or who have found intolerable the introduction of a rival, leading to ill-treatment by their husbands, are in nine cases out of ten Telugus. Again, the women whose character has been damaged by slander, the men who have lost their caste at the insinuation of others, are almost always Telugus complaining against Telugus, and that, be it remembered, in the midst of a population three parts Uriya.

I will not go so far as to say that facts like these prove the point on which I am insisting. Doubtless it may be urged that the Uriya is more ignorant, and therefore does not know what to do; is more indolent, and therefore does not care to come into court; is poorer, and therefore cannot afford the expense of a suit. It may be said that complaints are less frequent because morality is laxer. But I cannot subscribe to any of these reasons. The Uriya is not so ignorant, not so indolent, not so poor, but that he can come to court on matters which are often very trivial. There is nothing at all to point to a laxer morality. The only reasons besides those I have suggested which seem to me of any weight are these: that the Uriya woman is more loth to come into court, and that the parties are more easily reconciled. Both these reasons, however, are honourable to the Uriya, though in a different direction.

But while I cannot adduce any sufficient ethical reason, I must admit that there may be ethnical reasons which, if they do not fully explain these phenomena, at least contribute towards their explanation. It must be recorded that the Uriya woman guards herself very closely, like her Mahometan sister, and that necessity would be very strong which would drag her from her cherished seclusion before the gaze of unwonted eyes. It must be allowed that an insult in Uriya is not always accompanied by the pains of excommunication, and that a man may be content to hear himself called names, without fear that to-morrow he will not be able to obtain fire and water.

The Uriya, as I have found him, is particularly polite in small ways. I have expressed this opinion to several, and I have always heard that the Uriya is a rude and stupid brute. Now, there is an "open sesame!" to a man's polite feelings which can hardly be too highly estimated, and that is his language. The Uriya is highly delighted if he finds a European who can talk to him in his own language—perhaps it is partly because such Europeans are rare. He is—by hypothesis I was going to say—backward in the race of civilization; consequently he is timid. Therefore, if a man ride up and ask his way in Telugu of a man who does not know Telugu, he will probably get no answer! He will then ask, perhaps with a little bluster, and the terrified Uriya will run away!

In their dealings with foreigners the English are hardly celebrated as the politest of nations. The immortal Charles Yellowplush, Esq., has left us no very high opinion of the Frenchmen whom he met in Boulogne and of the "langwidges" they talked, while a later generation is contemporary with the Irish gentleman who could not control himself on hearing his mother called a "mare." It is hardly fair to blame the Uriya who, far from "scattering all the features" of anybody's face, simply stands stock still and, shall we say, grunts! If the shade of Demosthenes appeared before you and declaimed the "De Corona," he would hardly be justified in dealing you a clout on the head because you did not appreciate all his rhetorical finish!

If you talk, then, to the Uriya in Uriya you will generally find him polite. I have asked for the village officers, for some water for my horse, or the way to the next village, and plenty of willing men come to help me, while probably one or two will accompany me some distance. These are small things, but they are done cheerfully and politely; and I have known Uriyas put themselves to gratuitous inconvenience to do me some small service unasked.

I pass on from these inward and spiritual characteristics to the outward and visible signs, which may be more properly called customs. At first sight the dress of an Uriya man differs only from that of other natives by being dirtier; the dress of the women by being shorter. But here again I have noticed a distinction not altogether to the disadvantage of the Uriya men. All classes, even the lowest, wear the clothes wrapped *round* the loins, and tied in the way common to all natives of the better class in the north. The Telugu ryot, in the south of the district—and I may take him as a typical distinction—wears a string round the waist, on which he suspends his cloth, leaving the hips bare; and this mode of dress conveys rather the impression of undress. But whatever advantage the Uriya may gain in the style of his dress, he loses in the colour; and I fear the loss is far more prominent than the gain. It is very rare to see a white cloth, unless amongst the well-to-do classes: the ordinary cloth is of a dirty yellow colour. I have been told by an authority that both men and women anoint their bodies very copiously with saffron, in order to keep themselves cool; and I have been told that the men do so as much as the women. This use of saffron may account for the colour of the men's clothes, but I cannot unreservedly subscribe to the opinion I have just recorded. My own belief is that the women use saffron very largely as an adornment. But the colour of the clothes is probably due still more to the fact that they are not often sent to the professional washerman, "the dhobi," who makes things *white*. They are either washed at home, or at the period of the bath, the man merely exchanging his wet cloth for a dry one, and slightly rinsing the former. As the ordinary man and woman are ignorant of the refinements of the washerman's art, the result is not all that could be wished, and the cloth assumes a permanent muddy hue. This custom must be put down to the debit side of the Uriya's account.

But, in addition to this, the men have one peculiar custom in the matter of clothes, attributable to superstition, and not to economy. The cloth which they put on at meal-times never leaves the house; it is never washed by the washerman, but from time to time the women of the house rinse it in water. This is a curious custom, nor is it much to be applauded. It probably arises from that scrupulous dread of contamination which, carried to excess, seems to us so unreasonable in the matter of food of all kinds, but especially of water. But the remedy is worse than the disease, and their scrupulosity has only exemplified for them the "falsehood of extremes."

The mode of tying the turban is also peculiar.

The cloth is folded in such a way as to resemble the roof of a house, the head-dress being worn very high, and with a ridge running from front to back. The shape (which is not easy to describe) is really as distinct as the "cross-fold" of the Telugus, or the "pork-pie" or "inverted soup-plate" of others. In tying his turban the Uriya is very sedulous to display all its ornaments. In fact, however, this style of turban is not much seen. Most of the people wear no head-dress, and those who do, have for the most part adopted the fashion of their Telugu neighbours.

The clothes of the women are, as I have said, distinguished by their extreme brevity, and also by a copious use of saffron. The clothes are, however, not properly dyed, and the saffron is merely rubbed into them. The idea one gets is that they have been rolled about in a peculiar yellow mud, and have never been properly washed since. The saffron dye is therefore scarcely an improvement. Uriya women are particularly fond of colour. No woman will wear a cloth without a coloured border, though they do not much affect clothes coloured throughout. The kind of cloth most sought after is white, with a red border about two inches wide, and a deep band of red across its breadth. In the matter of borders the Uriya prefers to take a quantity rather than to be particular about the quality. The dress of the coolie class reaches only to the knees, and often not so low. The process of robing is very simple. The cloth is tied round the waist once, tucked in at one corner, and thrown over the shoulder once or twice, as its length may allow, and the toilette is complete—a somewhat simpler arrangement than the powders and patches, the unguents and perfumes of Belinda's bedroom. I speak, of course, only of those women whose modesty is not so delicate that it can bear neither the sun's rays nor the glances of others. Women who do not usually leave their own houses—women, that is to say, of the better class, wear the cloth reaching down to the ankles, and put on one with ampler folds, should they be called upon to leave the house at an unusual hour.

The Uriya women as a class are far more secluded than their Telugu sisters, and hence, when I say an unusual hour, I mean an hour of the day when others are about. An Uriya woman whose house does not afford her the means of performing her ablutions at home, goes out very early in the morning, say at four o'clock, to bathe, while lazy men are still slumbering.

Actaeon, on a like occasion, was turned into dog's meat for his presumption; but then, to be sure, Artemis was a goddess. Odysseus, on the other hand, received different treatment from Nausicaa. Which would be the fate in these days of the rash intruder into the village mysteries?

Uriya women, then, have a high sense of female modesty. It is not confined to the higher class alone. Even the women whom the necessities of life drive to work in the fields are exceptionally modest and respectful. A coolie woman will turn her face away from you, and, as you pass, she will draw her cloth more securely across her breast. I must put this down in her favour, if we contrast her with the Tamil women of the south, many of whom go about without shame, in no more clothing than their lords.

And while I am discussing this point, I may be pardoned for a slight digression regarding the Uriya notions of self-respect. There is one point on which nations, prominently, though in widely different ways, manifest their self-respect, and that is in their treatment of women. The Englishman who respects himself gives precedence in all points of etiquette to the lady. Among savage tribes no man will demean himself by doing work that his wife can do. The

Mahometan guards his wife and the female members of the family in the closest seclusion. And these feelings are reciprocal. The English lady and the savage wife would respect but little the man who did not conform to these customs; while, if the Mahometan lady were forced to present herself before the eyes of the world, she would be shamed and disgraced in her own eyes for ever, beyond all manner of speaking. I have pointed out earlier in this essay that the Uriya woman of the ryot class is kept in seclusion, and she will not go to work. That is the custom, and it is as definite as the European or the Mahometan customs are.

Famine was pressing heavily on the greater part of India in the year 1897, and Orissa had its share. It is in times like these that customs are emphasized. The Collector of the district talks of "foolish infatuation" when speaking of the reluctance of men to come to work. The expression is surely not correct. It is quite true that the men are reluctant to work under the famine rules, and that they will not send the women to work. The Uriya is naturally lazy, and he does not care to work if he can get on without it. Work in the fields, moreover, is everywhere regarded, even by the agricultural labourer, as in a higher grade of labour than breaking stones. It has been suggested to me that his refusal to work is due not to any feeling of self-respect, but solely to his natural indolence and to the influence of the caste heads, who hope to make a profit for themselves, by forcing the Government to give gratuitous relief in the village. For reasons of their own also, it is urged, they have commanded the people not to accept cooked food in kitchens. To be called "chotrokhya," or "eater in kitchens," is to be branded for life with the mark of Cain. We have all heard at one time or another of a sad story of the workhouse. We all know the dread an old couple have to "go upon the parish." Yet the old go to the workhouse only to die; the young leave it without friends to pity or despise them. But the Uriya "chotrokhya" goes back to the village in which he was born and bred. The old shake their heads at him; his friends with whom in happier days he, a naked urchin, made mud pies in the village street, now point at him the finger of scorn; the young shake off the dust of their feet against him. These things are admitted facts; they are customs, not of caste, but of race. There is absolutely nothing to show by whom and in what manner they were invented. It may be that sordid motives induce the people to continue a custom which higher feelings originated. It may be that a father, by refusing to work himself, or to allow his children to accept cooked food, finds it convenient to subsist on the grain granted in the village for the support of those children. If this is so, it is rather remarkable that a custom, founded on nothing but an elaborate fraud, and invented by the stupid Uriya, should not have been copied by his far more cunning Telugu neighbour.

But this is a long digression. I return to the dress and ornaments of the Uriya. Round the necks of the men is worn a curious sort of necklace made of beads. It has no intrinsic value, but it is supposed to be made of the "tulasi," the sacred plant. I am afraid that this is not always the case, and many necklaces are made of cocoanut and other woods; the Uriyas commit a pious fraud, if fraud it can be called. It is evident that since the necklace is made of the sacred plant it is connected with a religious rite. In fact, the strict Uriyas of a certain sect will not eat without their necklace, nor will they perform their devotions. It is not clear what was the origin of the custom, but if one may hazard a guess, perhaps it was originally the means of tying on an amulet. This theory is not altogether unsupported, for the Uriya often wears a golden necklace, called "dhanno-mali," from the resemblance of the beads to grains of rice. In the centre of this necklace is generally a small golden plate with the words "Sri ramo" engraved in Uriya on it. This points to its religious significance.

The only other peculiar ornament worn by males is a curious sort of gold earring. It is circular in shape, and it is almost always worn double, though the two parts are joined together. The best comparison that suggests itself is that of a double moon in the first quarter, with the horns produced in a circle till they meet. One would imagine this to be a very heavy ornament, but it is usually made of lac thinly plated over with gold. The earring is seldom made of solid metal.

The Uriya has not learned that beauty is "when unadorned adorned, the most," or else he is too conscious of the shortcomings of the women, for he loads them with ornaments in all available places: in the hair, in the nose, in the ears, on the neck, on the arms, from wrist to elbow, round the waist, and on the feet; jewels of silver and jewels of gold, works of brass and works of glass, beads and trinkets, rings and necklaces, bracelets and anklets—all are there in magnificent profusion. But such profusion is, of course, confined to the better classes. The wife of the ordinary ryot is content with perhaps nose and earrings; but, above all, she must have the silver and glass or brazen bracelets, often worn from wrist to elbow. This is a *sine qua non*; it takes the place of the wedding ring. No wife will be without her bracelets. Some castes, notably the working classes, prefer brass; others a profusion of colours in glass. As all the world knows, when a wife becomes a widow she takes off all her bracelets, except perhaps one, and that, if ornamented, is now beaten flat and defaced. And occasionally this symbol is used as the presentment of a counterfeit widowhood. For sometimes a woman who falls out with her husband, and is perhaps driven from her house, will solemnly break her bangles, in token that henceforth he is dead to her, that from that time she renounces him for ever.

To tell the truth, brass bracelets are a serious inconvenience. For the most part the brass is hollow, but the solid brass is very heavy. Mr. Maltby says that a set of these bangles will sometimes weigh as much as ten pounds. The glass bangles are but tawdry ornaments. They are made of lac, on a thin brass foundation, and covered over with a thin coating of glass. The earrings do not attract attention. The ears are not generally pulled down and disfigured as they are in the south, where lead is used to make the ear grow out of shape.

The house of the Uriya is usually a hut, made of mud dried in the sun. It is generally thatched with paddy straw, and is rectangular. The villages are built in more or less regular streets, but the direction of the main street must be east and west, and not north and south. In the building of their houses they observe one curious custom, though I am not sure that it is universal. They plough the land and sow in it some grain (generally black gram), after consulting a priest or seer. What the object of this is I have not been able to discover. One is reminded of the ancient custom of ploughing the lands before raising the walls of a city, and of the gift to Horatius, when

> " They gave him of the corn land
> That was of public right
> As much as two strong oxen
> Could plough from morn till night."

Sometimes, when a village is founded, a commemorative pillar is set up and adorned with coloured cloths and leaves, while the Brahmins call upon the god to bless the undertaking and propitiate him with sacrifices. Do we not even the same when some Royal personage goes to lay a foundation stone with a silver trowel, or float a ship by means of a button? "One touch of nature makes the whole world kin." The Brahmin becomes a lawn-sleeved bishop; the smoking sacrifice is turned into foaming champagne!

The Uriya is fond of smearing his house with red ochre, and will often adorn it with patterns done rudely in whitewash. Sometimes, however, if a native artist is available, a ground work of white is painted on the red ochre, and on this a picture—it may be of fightings among the gods—of huntings and other devices. Thus the ignorant Uriya ryot is not without his standard of beauty, is not ignorant of fresco, and imitates in his rude way the walls of the house of Glaucus and the convent of San Marco. To a European eye these things are not ornaments. To those who look for the face and form of Nature in art, gods with blue faces and six arms, impossible men on impossible horses, and all other fabled monsters, are matters rather of curiosity than of pleasure. The doorways show very fair carving, not, however, of figures, but generally of rosettes, arabesques, and other conventional patterns.

It is curious that the Uriyas seem to love being filthy so much, that they thrust their dirtiness upon every chance comer. To him whose ideas were nurtured in the west, it seems natural to clean the outside of the cup and platter at least, to welcome the stranger to his best, and to keep in the background his kitchen and his stables—all that is unclean or unseemly. On the threshold of an Uriya house is the cattle shed, with its accumulated filth and straw lying around. Beyond this, but generally entirely separate from it, is the cooking and dining room; behind this again, the sleeping apartments. In these matters, except that he is content with a minimum of space, I am not aware that the Uriya materially differs from other native races; details would therefore only be wearisome.

The hills and the jungles, by which the Uriya is surrounded from his birth, have made him naturally a keen sportsman, and I have never had any trouble in getting beaters for my various shooting expeditions. They seem to take great interest in the sport, and are highly delighted at a successful issue. That their love for sport is not merely the love of the hire or of the meat which may fall to their share, I am fully convinced. The tom-toms play equally loudly the funeral march of a bear and a deer. As for bears, they are averse to killing them, as they have a curious fancy that the souls of their ancestors inhabit the bodies of bears after leaving their human prison. They will not themselves take the risk of injuring their ancestors, though they do not seem to mind another man doing so. Their solicitude is, therefore, subjective rather than objective. From time immemorial men have loved to hunt and to shoot, not merely for the sake of the meat, but also, and chiefly, for the pleasure and excitement of the chase. It would be strange, therefore, if the Uriya, who is only half civilized, did not take a pleasure in these sports. I was surprised, however, at my last bear hunt to find the accountant of the village with me—not standing afar off; and if he was not in at the death, the sharp stones that cut his naked feet were to blame, and not his eagerness.

The Uriya is not fond of education. He cultivates his mind as little as his fields. He is content to sow one crop if that will be enough for his subsistence. He is content with his own low standard of comfort, though a very little more labour, either manual or mental, would enable him to rise above it. The consequence is that he seldom climbs beyond the heights of the Upper Primary Examination. The two channels into which those who have received higher education are almost sure to drift, are Government service and the law. The number of Uriyas in the higher grades of the magisterial or ministerial service of Government might be counted on the fingers of one hand. I have only seen *one* Uriya pleader, and he was a retired Government servant. I am not at all sure that this has not its advantage. In the south hosts of would-be Government servants wander about in search of work, and swell the number of the unemployed. The immense supply of vakils * creates an immense demand. To go to law is one of the luxuries of the people and their chiefest recreation. There are even gradations in the luxury, and between a civil suit before the district judge, or a criminal case before the native magistrate, lie all the gradations that there are between a box at a theatre and a seat in the pit—stalls, dress circle, and upper circle all have their analogy. But this is not a healthy form of recreation. If two ryots fight, it is better for them to settle the affair in their own way, or, if they must come to court, to come themselves and tell their

* Native attorneys.

story, than that there should be all the usual wire drawing, and hair splitting, and purse straining, while

"Raman pays that pleaders' clerks may dine."

On the other hand, the very low state of education in most rural villages is not only a drawback to the administration, but to the people themselves. Seeing that districts are made up of taluks,* and taluks are composed of village units, it is essential to good administration that the officers of the village should be intelligent and capable; and this, emphatically, the Uriya village officers are not.

But, though the village officers are a thorn in the side of the Government authorities, it is in a far wider way that the general lack of education produces evil results. For in very many cases the karnam or accountant is the only man in the village who can write more than his name. The king of the village is the lord of the pen. For the king of the village is master of the Treasury, and the pen is the golden key. Every ryot who pays money knows that he should get a "rasid," † and knows that a "rasid" is a bit of paper with writing on it. But to very few are the figures and letters, and still more the English calendar,

* Divisions. † Receipt.

anything more than cabalistic characters to be taken for granted.

I have endeavoured to find out something about the games of the Uriyas, and more especially the out-door games; but I could not discover much. The little naked children appear to play in the dust, or chase each other about without any rules, as it does not seem right for boys over fifteen to play at all. And while I am talking about these children, I may mention that Uriya boys dispense with clothes for a very long time. Boys of ten and eleven run about the villages absolutely naked, save for what I may call a proleptic string round the waist. The children of the ordinary peasant class have too much to do—washing the bullocks, driving away the birds from the ripening paddy, and doing a hundred and one odd jobs in the paddyfield—to invent out-door games for themselves. And, after all, in the matter of their out-door games the Anglo-Saxon race stands alone in the world. One game they have, however, for the special festival of Sravana Pournami, or the full moon of August-September. In almost every village you will notice a curious mound of earth in the shape of a wedge, the thick end being about six feet from the ground. At the thick end a pole is put up, and from the pole is hung a bunch of flowers. The game is to run up the wedge and jump over the thick end of it, taking on the way the flowers, which are hung so high as to necessitate a fair jump. Not a very exciting game one would think, but competition adds zest to any game, and perhaps some annas change hands over the various competitors—and there is no stimulant like betting.

But if there are no outdoor games, there are plenty played indoors. Most of these are variations of games played on boards divided into so many squares, and to describe them would be simply like writing out a series of those "directions" which are to be found in every parlour game of the kind. One of the commonest of these games is the "tiger and sheep," corresponding to our "fox and geese." The names indicate very well the direction in which the fears of eastern and western farmers run.

I was walking down the main street of one of the larger villages one day, when I noticed two men playing chess. I went up to look at the game, and found, as indeed I expected, that they play this game as we play it. The queen, however, is not allowed—on the principle perhaps of the Zenana; she becomes the minister or mantiri. The bishop is turned into a mere camel. The knight is merged in his own horse —perhaps the nobler animal of the two, while the castle is, appropriately enough, changed into an elephant. But if Uriyas are not addicted to outdoor games, there is one joyful ceremony at which all let themselves loose in a wild sort of blind man's buff, and that is marriage.

In the peculiarity of their marriage customs the Uriyas are no whit behind other nations. Perhaps of all recorded instances the Sabine ladies were married in the most primitive fashion, the one-tenth of the law which is not possession being somewhat disregarded in their case. Even amongst the later Romans the marriage was a pure contract, and the wife was as much a member of the *familia* as the freed men or the slaves. We ourselves have many curious customs, symbolical and fantastic. The bride is veiled and wears white; the token of marriage is a gold ring on the third finger of the left hand; there is a particular kind of cake, and the young couple are sent on their journey with showers of rice and old shoes. Therefore, after the cake and the old shoes, let no one laugh at the apparent frivolity of some of the Uriya customs.

Different castes have different customs. Amongst

the Brahmins this solemn ceremony begins with what must really be considered a rough-and-tumble game! The bridegroom stands behind a screen in the court-yard. The bride comes out of her chamber, and throws three handfuls of salt and rice at him. Then there is a scramble amongst the guests, the bride's party trying to get some grains of salt, and the bride-groom's doing their best to prevent this by trampling it into the ground. If the bride's followers are so lucky as to get hold of some grains, they keep them against the day of the marriage dinner, when they are served in the bridegroom's plate. If he eats them he loses in the estimation of his wife's relatives.

This sounds like a pure game, and to this the custom seems to have degenerated. Probably the main idea is that the bridegroom's duty is to protect his wife, and not to receive from her. As salt and rice are the common necessaries of Hindu life, the bride tempts the bridegroom by offering these symbols of all sustenance to him. And since it is degrading for the man to receive support from the woman, it is degrading for him to eat his wife's rice and salt, which are typical of this support. I must admit that this is conjecture; but probably every custom has an origin, and this solution seems at least likely.

Another trial which the bridegroom has to undergo is the ordeal of the Mantapam. In this ordeal the bridegroom sits on a flat stone, while the bride's relatives—"the virgins that bear her company"—do their best to upset him. It does not appear that he gains any credit by overcoming them, while, if they upset him, he is held up to ridicule. This is rather a one-sided way of doing things, and the bridegroom, if he has a sturdy set of amazons to deal with, may well find his position rather precarious.

If I mistake not, this has its origin in the same idea as the custom I have lately recounted. The point of view is perhaps slightly changed, and the husband appears as the champion, instead of the bread winner. He must prove that he is physically capable of upsetting his enemies. It may be that since the contest is with his wife's *female* relatives, some idea of moral strength is intended to be typified; but as the contest is purely a physical contest, I do not think this is probable. It is, however, possible that the part of the ceremony where physical force is used is symbolical of the more primitive form of marriage by capture.

When the ceremony is over the bridal pair return home, where they find a great pile of stools and cooking pots. These the bridegroom kicks over. The bride gathers them together, and piles them up again. The bridegroom, rather wilfully one would think, kicks them over again—and this is repeated three times. On the surface the lesson we seem to see here is that of patience. The bride is given a foretaste of what she may expect when she has her domestic cares to look to. I think, however, the custom means to imply that henceforth the wife is to be careful and troubled about domestic matters; that she is to be in subjection to her husband, and possibly also that she must patiently submit to his moods. This would account for the laborious piling up of these articles—the labour of Sisyphus, though fortunately not without end; but I cannot explain why the husband should kick the pots down, unless it is to show that he is master in his own household, and can do as he likes.

While the marriage ceremony continues the bridegroom may not eat cold food, nor salt, nor certain vegetables, in his father-in-law's house. This appears to be a very whimsical custom, and the meaning of it is not obvious on the surface. It is possible that the husband is warned not to place himself in dependence upon his wife's relatives. I am, however, inclined to think that, since cold food would not usually be offered to chance guests, but only to members of the household, and since from the earliest ages the eating of a man's salt creates an inviolable tie, the custom arises from the sense that it is indecent for the bridegroom to instal himself as a member of the family before he is entitled to do so by a more definite connection.

Every day at dinner the betrothed couple play at cowries. The bridegroom takes these and throws them on the ground. The bride collects them and puts them again into his hand. This is repeated seven times, for the numbers three and seven seem to be considered the complete numbers by most Oriental nations. The bridegroom then holds the cowries in his tightly closed fist, and the bride has to open his hand. Then her turn comes, and the bridegroom has to open her hand. This game seems to have no significance whatever. It is merely a little diversion in the somewhat tedious eight days' ceremony.

When the time arrives for the bride to join her husband, she proceeds to his house, where she is met by her husband's sister, the custodian of the gate, who refuses her admittance. This she has to purchase by presenting a "sari," or fine cloth, to the inexorable dame. I imagine that this is supposed to represent the unwillingness with which the bridegroom's sister leaves her station as mistress of the house. Not until she receives a sufficient reward will she hand over the keys of her trust. Of course now the resistance is feigned and the reward is nominal. We have often read of old retainers who have been much disconcerted by the taking unto themselves of wives by their masters, until then thought to be confirmed old bachelors.

If the husband has no sister, the part is acted by another woman. As the custom is purely symbolical and has lost its original meaning, it matters little who takes the part, just as among ourselves it is a matter of small moment who gives the bride away.

Yet another ordeal is before the wife before she enters upon her domestic reign. A golden ring is thrown into a pot of rice and water, and she has to fish the ring out. Her success or failure is taken as an omen of the measure of her success in the duties of housekeeping. This finding of the ring is very closely analogous to the boiling of a ring in the Christmas pudding. I cannot find that the custom had any origin except in superstition, and it must be ranked with the "Sortes Virgilianae," and others of that kind.

The Uriyas are scrupulously particular regarding the exposure of the bride to the gaze of her male relatives. All possible precautions are taken. She does not stir out, unless compelled to do so. Even then she walks by unfrequented paths, and is closely enveloped in a veil. Further, she must not pronounce the names of her husband or his parents, or his relatives of the ascending line. Nay, more; she must even avoid words of which the first syllable corresponds with the first syllable of any of these names. She may not speak to them, but must express herself by signs. This is slavery! The custom, the strict observance of which we may be permitted to doubt, may have had its origin in a transition from polyandry to monogamy or polygamy. The husband's brothers, who would formerly have shared the wife with him, would be of all men most to be avoided. I am not, however, aware that the Uriyas ever practised polyandry. However the custom arose, it is now overlaid with monstrous additions, and demonstrates, if not the falseness, at least the absurdity—one might say the cruelty—of extremes. The idea of decent respect, which was enjoined by a few salutary rules of conduct, is now obscured by a multitude of senseless customs, so that the respectful and respected matron now appears so abject as to be a slave, so frail as to be unworthy of her husband's confidence.

I proceed to notice one or two customs peculiar to less important castes :—

Kaivartas (fishermen).—These men have to marry their daughters before the age of puberty ; if they fail to find a husband in time, the girl must be married to an arrow.

Ghasis (scavengers).—An earthen vessel filled with water is suspended from the marriage booth. On the last day but one of this protracted wedding the bridegroom breaks the vessel. The bride's brother then strikes him on the back, and the bridegroom leaves the house in mock anger. Next day the bride goes to his house and invites him back.

Rellis (or gardeners).—The bridegroom, with the permission of the village magistrate, marches straight into the bride's house and ties the wedding necklace round her neck. A gift of seven and a half rupees and a pig to the caste men, and of five rupees to the bride's father, completes this very primitive ceremony.

I have merely selected a few amongst the many castes which have marriage customs peculiar to themselves. I have given the customs without comment, and explanations will doubtless occur to the reader. They serve as illustrations of the many apparently senseless ceremonies with which the simple marriage contract may be overlaid.

We read of the famous Solomon Grundy that he was born on Monday, and after a rapid career met his death on Saturday. With no less speed must we fly from the rejoicings of the marriage booth to the wailings of the death chamber.

In the general character of their funerals the Uriyas do not differ from other Hindu races. Distinctions are only to be found in matters of detail. Upon the death of the head of the household the body is carried to the burning ground by the male relatives; the eldest son leads the way, carrying a broken pitcher with fire in it. The women remain behind to console the widow, and to add their lamentations to hers. Meanwhile, if the deceased be a rich man, the route of the procession is marked by a line of copper coins and fried rice—largesses which are thrown into the road, not apparently to any specific persons, but simply for him who will to appropriate.

It is, I suppose, an act of general charity, designed to speed the departed spirit on its journey to the other world. On arrival at the burning ground the body is washed and wrapped in a new cloth. It is then laid on the pyre, with the head to the north. The eldest son walks three times round the pyre, murmuring prayers or *mantrams* and burning *kusa* grass. This he thrusts into the pyre beneath the head of the corpse, and at once makes his way homeward—nor must he look back.

The widow and the female relatives then go to the nearest tank, where the former breaks her bracelets.

On the fourth day the son collects the ashes, with intent to lay them at a more convenient season in the bosom of Mother Ganges. The next few days are occupied in feasting, but on the tenth day all the relatives, both male and female, assemble at a tank. The men are shaved there, and the women have their nails pared. The ceremony of purification follows. Men and women bathe and put on new clothes. The widow is given a borderless *sari*, or cloth, the sign of her widowhood. The whole ceremony of funerals lasts for twelve days.

In all this there is, I believe, very little that is

not common, at any rate with unimportant variations, to other Hindu races. I have therefore given only a rapid sketch of the ceremony, in order to introduce some of the more important details which are peculiar to Uriyas. It has been the custom from time immemorial to regard shaving the head and face as a sign of decent mourning. The Hindus are essentially a conservative race, and we are fortunate in possessing the records of an ancient Oriental tribe, which, whatever may be their historical value, explain, and are explained by, the manners and customs of Oriental races of to-day. Thus Job, when he heard of all his disasters—the loss of all his wealth and the death of his sons— "took water and shaved himself." And since it is a shame for a woman to shave her head, and since she does not, for obvious reasons, shave her face, the paring of the nails is substituted, not, I think, because it has any significance in itself, but simply that the women may also partake with the men in their ceremonial observances; it is, as it were, the symbol of a symbol.

In an earlier part of this essay I alluded to the love which Uriya women have for colours. It is evident that the assumption by the widow of a plain white *sari* arises from the same feelings which prompt English people to wear black, or induced the old Athenians to put on violet. And though I believe that Uriya women are fond of colour for its own sake, yet, since a cloth without a border is the distinctive sign of widowhood, it is natural that the women should insist on borders to their clothes. Amongst us black crape is a distinctive sign of mourning, and it is not worn save by those who are in mourning.

Various little peculiarities of detail are to be met with in the twelve-days' ceremony. The bearers of the corpse, at whatever hour the burning takes place, must wait until the hour of sunset or sunrise before leaving the ground, according as the man died during the day or night. On the second day the relatives sit down to a meal of bitterness (Uriya, *Pitákhiyá*) made of *margosa* leaves. The significance of this is fairly clear. The real ceremony of mourning seems to last for nine days only, for on the tenth day we find that the mourners—except perhaps the chief among them—go to a tank, there bathe, then on their return wash their feet in turmeric water, and enter the house through a new booth put up for the purpose. Washing the feet is of course an ordinary symbol of purification. I suppose the booth is meant to mark their re-entry into the affairs of the world after their nine days' seclusion. It is made more clear that the actual funeral ceremony lasts only nine days, by the fact that on the tenth day, and not before, the use of ghee, oil, and chillies is allowed. During the whole twelve days, however, a sacred lamp is kept burning in a small hole in the corner of the room. And if the relatives end their days of mourning on the tenth day, the eldest son has still a mysterious rite to perform. In the darkness of the eleventh night he rises and, taking with him a palm branch, a piece of *kora* wood, and a new earthen vessel, he makes his way to a tank or to an unfrequented place. There he strips himself naked, mutters some incantations over the things he has brought, and throws them away. This done, he returns home. I suppose that every rite and ceremony has a meaning, either practical or symbolical, and perhaps one may discover a meaning in the drawing apart of the young man, and in the self-humiliation of his nakedness. But it is hard to find a reason why he takes the branch, and the wood, and the pot, or why he throws them away. Perhaps, like the Greek *obol* for Charon, they represent the necessaries with which the spirit must be furnished on its way to the other world.

Unfortunately, though these ceremonies are harmless enough, the Uriyas have one custom which contravenes all the laws of sanitation. They refuse to burn or bury the victims of cholera or small-pox, but the corpses are simply taken and thrown outside the village. The origin of such a superstition is not far to seek. The goddess who presides over the disease has laid her hand upon the victim, and he is thenceforth accursed. It is sacrilege to offend the goddess by offering the body the decent rites of interment or cremation. So it is left to poison the air, and the souls of many men go down to Hades lest the goddess should be offended. Not more certain victims to a fanatic idea were those sacrificed to the war god of the Aztecs, or those immolated less directly in honour of the Virgin, in the holocausts of the Inquisition.

III.

RELIGION.

I FIND nothing remarkable in the religious system of the Uriyas. They have the same general belief in the Hindu theology as most natives of the same class. But that is not saying much. Unable to conceive of the Deity as an essential being, omnipresent, omnipotent, yet always invisible, they are obliged to satisfy their yearning for the concrete by journeys to Puri, and, still more, by the worship of the village goddess. Though they ascribe the seasons and the varying natural phenomena to the *Poromeswaro*, or Supreme Being, I do not think that the word conveys any definite impression to their minds.

Of Puri, the famous shrine of Jagannath, lying, however, in Orissa proper, this is not the place to give any detailed description. But though the place itself may be beyond the scope of this essay, yet the influence it exercises upon the people is so great, and the journey thither in some respects so curious, as to merit a passing glance.

It is about the month of July that one may observe crowds of devotees flocking in or from the direction of Puri, their hair, coloured to all shades of brown and yellow, fantastically piled upon their heads; their bodies smeared with the grey ash, which would make them look uncanny, if the generally substantial appearance of the individual did not rather give the impression of mere uncleanliness. Their impedimenta are few; they wear practically no clothes. A string of beads round the neck, a wallet, a brass pot, an antelope skin for sleeping and sitting on, and the indispensable snuff-box are the only articles they carry. The pilgrim would be merely an object of curiosity if he were not a pest. We may admire the length of the locust's leg or the structure of his wing, until the green field is a bare desert, and then we curse the insect. We may look curiously at the devotee, but he brings with him the terrible scourge of an outbreak of cholera. He is as ill-omened as the locust.

The journey from Rambha on the Chilka lake is generally performed in large flat-bottomed boats. The sails are made of bamboo mats, such as are used for the covering of native carts. One may well imagine that such a boat, with a mat stuck on a pole for its "white wings," is a clumsy, slow-moving affair enough. The lake has a local god, a presiding deity of its own, who must be propitiated with offerings of plantains, of rice, of flowers. Woe betide the impious man who neglects these offerings! The angry god churns the waters, stirring them as one stirs a pot, and the unlucky boat sinks in the whirlpool. One has heard of such a god even in England. "Now, to this day on the river Trent, the Nottingham bargemen, when the river is in a certain flooded state (a kind of eddying swirl it has) call it eager. 'Have a care, there is the eager coming;'" a very real giant, in fact an ogre.

Uriya temples are modelled upon the great temple at Puri, and have outwardly very little in common with the great temples of the south. The temple at Puri—the Mecca of the Hindus on the east coast—is dedicated to Vishnu, as Jagannath, whose famous car was once said to have immolated so many devoted victims and sent them, let us hope, by a short and easy road to heaven. In consequence of this temple, most of the Uriyas in Ganjam are worshippers of Vishnu, generally under the title of Radhakrishna, or of

Jagannath. The more awful Siva, the destroyer, is worshipped with fear and trembling upon the outskirts of towns and villages. He is not represented by any graven image; but in the symbol of a single pillar of granite, the devout recognize the presence of Divinity. His temples are not carven, but he is generally lodged in a rude house, with mud walls and roofed with thatch. Such a house I have seen with walls dilapidated and roof in ruins, hidden away in the heart of a bamboo jungle. Yet thither flock the people, to worship in sunshine or in rain, in time of famine or in time of plenty, careless of distance, fatigue, or discomfort. It is difficult to say why such a terrible god is housed in so poor a dwelling. But the ark of God contained nothing but the tables of the law; and long after the final conquest of Canaan, David complained that the ark of the Lord dwelt "within curtains," while he was lodged in a house of cedar.

The temple of Vishnu, under whatever names he may be adored, is built in three parts, corresponding, if I may say so without straining analogy, to the three parts of our cathedrals. The inner apartment is the abode of the god himself, the Holy of Holies, into which the priest alone may enter; and this corresponds to our altar. The next part of the temple is the chancel, where the worshippers congregate to offer up their prayers and to deposit their sacrifices—a bunch of plantains, some flowers, or a handful of rice. The outer part is the nave, where the congregation sing hymns after their orisons are over.

As every one knows, the Hindu god is completely anthropomorphic. He lives with his wife, and often with a servant; he indulges in the purely human delights of dining and of bathing. "Peradventure," also, "he sleepeth," and, like his fellow divinity, he often goes on a journey; and to the people these are all very serious realities. Even the Brahmins, who are generally allowed into the innermost sanctuary, are kept without the veil during the sacred hour of the banquet. I once asked the people to let me see the inside of the temple. They were not at all offended, but, after they had made inquiries, they told me politely that the god had not yet had his bath, and was not prepared to receive visitors, but if I would call again in an hour or two I might then expect to be received! This temple was sacred to Rama Sita and their servant Hanumán.

That the journey of the god is a reality it does not take the bloody car of Jagannath to prove;

those are my witnesses who have seen a car festival, where crowds of men are tugging at the cables and painfully dragging the heavy car up the long street.

The most striking feature of the Uriya temple,* seen from the outside, is the great Holy of Holies. This is built in the shape of a barrel, and is crowned by a fluted roof and, over all, a pinnacle. This barrel stands high above the rest of the temple, and is built according to fixed proportions laid down by the Silpi Shastra, the height bearing a fixed ratio to the area. The other rooms allotted to the worshippers are not striking, but they are generally adorned with carvings, and the roof is a succession of more or less artistic terraces. The temple is very compact; there are none of the courtyards and outlying fanes to which one becomes accustomed in the south. Beyond the three rooms of the temple, and a cook-room or so, there is nothing.

The inside is distinctly disappointing. There are no carvings and no ornaments. In the temple which I was allowed to enter, I saw nothing but plaster, once white, but now coloured to various shades of brown and black by the smoke and soot of evil-smelling

* I am, of course, speaking of the ordinary temples in moderate-sized villages, of which the one described is a fair type.

lamps and unshaded candles. A priest lit a lamp or a torch, and there loomed through the darkness a white sheet spread over a table. Gradually to one's accustomed eyes some black masses upon this altar took the shape of ten or twelve dolls seated in a row. These were the deities of the place, and their average height was about a foot and a half. Except for the idols, which were, of course, the *raison d'être* of the whole edifice, and, therefore, could scarcely be excluded, the simplicity, though not the cleanliness of the place, must have won the heart of the sternest of Scotch Covenanters.

In the matter of food—those washings of cups, and pots, and brazen vessels, which, in the eyes of the Hindu, as in the eyes of the Pharisees, are so intimately connected with religion—the Uriyas have their own distinctive peculiarities. Unlike their more austere southern brethren, not only the higher castes of Sudras, but Brahmins themselves eat fish and, I have been told, the flesh of wild animals, such as the boar, the deer, or the antelope. They do not, however, touch domestic animals. The following was the reason given why Brahmins are allowed to take animal food. Rama, while he was wandering in the north, through Orissa, sought hospitality, and did not seek in vain. The houses were thrown open to him, and the fare, sumptuous or frugal, according to the means of the host, was shared with him. But when he journeyed to the south the houses were shut against him. He sought rest and food, and found none; he asked for hospitality, and was refused. Therefore he blessed those who had entertained angels unawares, and cursed the Brahmins of the south, that they should no more eat meat. I give this story with diffidence, as having received it at second hand. It is perhaps fair to ascribe it to the vanity or imagination of the Uriya Brahmin who told it.

But while the Brahmin is allowed this latitude in the matter of his food, and while all other castes also are free to eat meat without fear of ex-communication, all castes except the very lowest abstain from the fowl and the pig; and not only from the fowl, but also from eggs. There is, of course, a perfectly natural explanation for this. The pig and the fowl are the most unclean of all the unclean animals to be met with in an Indian village. The law was evidently in the original a rule of health, and, like so many other laws of the same kind, the ceremonial has remained and the meaning is lost. I suppose that every intelligent reader of the book of Leviticus must have noticed that though the animals which were declared unclean were classed under a general principle, yet those mentioned as examples are certainly amongst the beasts from which one would instinctively abstain. If you were to ask an Uriya why he does not eat a fowl, he would of course simply say that it was against the rules of his caste. His philosophy is content with that explanation, and does not seek to question the wisdom of his forefathers. The egg, of course, goes with the fowl, being of the same nature, and the only thing which is surprising is that a people who live in the midst of uncleanliness, and who drink water that the very animals refuse, should consent to be so strictly governed by a superstitious scruple, based upon a sanitary law.

Of superstition, as distinct from religion, there is no lack. It is natural that a people whose civilization is still undeveloped, and whose education is yet in earliest infancy, should hold fast to a faith in divination, witchcraft, and in ghosts. Professor Huxley, in an interesting essay called "The Evolution of Theology," has shown that every religion has its stage of ghost worship, or, at least, of belief in ghosts, as well as in the supernatural power exercised by certain persons over them. The evolution of the Uriya theology has not, it would seem, advanced beyond this stage.

A certain young girl was suffering from some mental disease, and was described by those who knew her as "having a devil." The words are clearly used in the same sense in which they are used in the Scriptures. It does not appear precisely what this devil was, but it was probably some form of seizure. In due course she was put under the care of a native doctor. While under his treatment she is said to have given vent to a sort of ecstatic utterance, and to have declared that she was bewitched by a certain man. Whether the girl really accused the man—whether she did so acting under natural and not divine influence, or whether the doctor, to satisfy a private grudge, thus interpreted an inarticulate cry—these are points which are not determined. The priestess of Delphi herself sometimes proved that she, too, was of like passions with ourselves, and gave expression to ideas for which Apollo was certainly not responsible.

At any rate, the utterance in question was at once ascribed to the devil, who, in the course of exorcism, had thus revealed his identity. The exclamation was supernatural, and therefore infallible. The man must be brought out and cured of this terrible power of the evil eye. Accordingly the friends and relatives of the girl banded together and went to this man's house. They broke in; they dragged him out into the road; they laid him on his back, and sat on his chest. They then proceeded to extract his two front teeth with a hammer and pinchers in the most deliberate manner, using the hammer probably as one would use it for loosening a nail! The object of this was to prevent the exercise of the magic. It does not appear how the cure was to work—whether the operators thought that the words of cursing or of magic, coming through the orifice of the teeth, would be mumbled, and thus lose some of their incisive force, and therefore of their power for evil, or whether it was thought that the devil wanted room to fly out. Perhaps they thought that the charm lay in the teeth, as the strength lay in Samson's hair, or that the magic was stored up behind the teeth, like the poison of the cobra. It is probable, however, that the first of these explanations is the true one.

Does not such a scene transport us back to the Middle Ages? Does it not remind us of the ducking-stool and the over-zealous shrew? Perhaps soon some enterprising Uriya headman will institute a Star Chamber, or an Inquisition in his village pound, to be named from some monstrous fiends on his wall—productions of a local artist!

A more horrible instance follows. At a village only about eight miles from Berhampore, the chief town of the district, was committed a deed recalling the barbarities of the Mexican savages, who, combining religion with a fine sense of utility and economy, slew before the war-god their human victims, and ate them themselves afterwards! True, in the present instance the cannibal feast was left out of the programme! The *dramatis personæ* were ordinary villagers, mainly of the artisan class. They were also worshippers of the goddess, as was the victim in this "village tragedy." On a certain night they all went out together. By-and-bye, according to a preconcerted plan, one of the party suggested a drink. The intended victim was drugged and taken along to the statue of the goddess, or, at least, to the shrine containing what did duty for the statue. He was there thrown down with his face to the ground, in an attitude suggesting supplication, and while he was still in a state of stupor, his head was chopped off with a native axe. The pure savagery of the action was enhanced by the inhumanity of using an instrument so imperfectly adapted to the work it was called upon to do.

There is no doubt that in this instance the sacrifice was made in perfect good faith. It calls to our remembrance the Meriah sacrifices of the Khonds, those Moloch offerings to the earth goddess, whose gift of fertility was to be won only by the outpouring of an innocent victim's blood. Yet, with all the horror of a Meriah sacrifice—since human nature must recoil from human torture—it was not without its poetic ceremonial. In the present instance no garlands bedecked the victim; no priest consecrated him to the Earth Mother. He was slaughtered as one would slaughter an ox. The dark goddess needed only the blood of a human sacrifice, and was not to be appeased with ceremonial.

I pass from this gruesome relic of barbarian times to the more mediæval belief in accredited diviners. These people work a great deal of mischief, but it is certain that the people believe in them. Indeed, the mischief they do is the direct result of the credulity. A man once lost some paddy or some trifling vessel from his house. Not being able to find it, he sallied forth in quest of the oracle—which in this case was many miles away. What the votive offering was, history does not record. Probably, however, the utterances of the Sanyasi * were not priced as highly as the ecstasies of Apollo's Delphic priestess. At any rate, the inquirer obtained the information he wanted, couched, of course, in mysterious language, and straightway he accused one of his near relations. Hinc lacrymae! for the latter, not choosing to part so cheaply with his reputation, promptly charged him with defamation. The simple fellow relied upon the word of the god-inspired, but, alas! the god was in angry mood, or perhaps the less divine impulse of self-preservation prevailed. The right reverend proved but a broken reed; the soothsayer denied his soothsaying!

I have been told, however, of cases in which these people have really discovered facts of which they could have had no previous knowledge; I give this for what it is worth. Unfortunately the age is sceptical of miracles; the saints themselves are relegated to the class of "Sludge the medium;" and where the information is at second hand some allowance must be made for the personal equation.

* Ascetic.

A more interesting kind of divination, or, at least, of supernatural agency, was discovered in one of the remoter villages of the district. It is in the leafy month of September, when the trees are dressed in their gayest, that a motley crowd of men, women, and children may be seen wending their way to the little village of Nuagada, to witness, if not to take part in, a curious ceremony. The scenery lends its aid in heightening the effect of the romantic rite. Nestling in the arms of the hills, the village lies hidden from sight in the midst of feathery bamboo, and completely surrounded by a natural moat. The place is idyllic; one can wander at will through grove on grove of bamboo, relieved here by a clump of aloes, there by a tamarind or a banyan-tree, while ever underneath murmurs the running streamlet, and the silence of the glades is broken only by the cry of the jungle-fowl, and the softer cooing of the green pigeon. It is in such a scene as this that is performed the mysterious rite to which the people flock. A holy man comes forth, a fire is kindled—no small fire of twigs, but a blaze of jungle faggots, the flames leaping up breast high. Through this the inspired walks unharmed, and proceeds to take his seat on a pile of sharp, strong thorns, raised about two feet from the ground and woven in the form of a stool about two feet square. This is the crucial test. So lightly clad as to be almost naked, he takes his seat on this forbidding throne. If he is truly inspired, the thorns will break beneath him, or will be turned aside, powerless to pierce his divinely protected skin. But woe unto that man into whom the true god has not entered! Not for him will the thorns fall away harmless; he shall taste to the full the bitterness of his presumption. And the punishment is not a light one! Let any sceptical reader twine for himself such a seat of strong bamboo thorns; let him clothe himself in the raiment or non-raiment of a fakir, and take his seat. I think neither he nor his scepticism will remain long.

Securely seated upon his thorny throne, and wielding a knife or axe, the god-inspired now proceeds to answer the requests of the many who have come from far and near to inquire of the oracle. And to each one in turn come with appropriate gestures the answers, "voces, responsa sibyllae." Promises of offspring to women, promises of cure to the sick, promises of relief to the distressed: these and much more does the god grant to his subjects for a consideration; for he is a very practical god. Not even the indulgences which Luther denounced were bought and sold more shamelessly than the promises and prophecies of this mercenary divinity. Nor is the god himself absent from the rite. It is said that long ages ago at one of these ceremonies he took, like Saturn, to devouring his own children. History has not recorded whether he did so out of pure delight, from feelings of vengeance, or as a just retribution. Perhaps the people ventured to do unlawful things, and were burnt up, as the fire in the hands of Korah and Abiram proved their undoing. Perhaps they had rashly gazed on the face of Him who was too holy for profane eyes. Even Moses and Elijah in the old legends dared not look upon the face of the Lord. At any rate the sequel in this case is rather ludicrous. The god is allowed on sufferance. He is placed with his back to the people—not taking up his position as the Merciful One, who is hiding his unbearable splendour, but put in the corner like a naughty child for fear he should get into mischief!

But of the power of his prophecies and promises he gives some very practical illustrations. He will take his trusting suppliants through the fire, and they will not be burned; he will cut them with his knife, and the blood will refuse to flow; he will seat them on the thorns, and they will do them no harm.

All this is clearly the relic of a barbarous rite. Perhaps it would be more accurate to say that it is the imitation of rites still practised among the aboriginal tribes, but without the grosser barbarities common amongst the latter. The curious part of this rite is that the promises are practical, capable of proof and of disproof. The Delphic oracle was notorious for its ambiguities; Crœsus was told that he would destroy a great nation; Pyrrhus obtained the even more famous hedging answer—

"Aio te Romanos vincere posse."

The indulgences certainly found credit, but no one was in a position to prove their efficacy, for obvious reasons.

The present case reminds one of the miracles of the Old Testament. "Go, wash in Jordan seven times," said Elisha, "and thou shalt be clean." Here is a man who might strike his hand over the place and recover the leper.

"Here is the finger of God; a flash of the will that can,
Existent behind all laws, that made them, and, lo! they are."

For the people believe in him. Year after year gives them ample opportunity for testing the truth of his prophecies, and year after year they flock to him in their hundreds. After this who shall say that the age of miracles is past?

Powerful as is the benign god for good, still more powerful is the vengeance of the offended deity. Wishing to look at the thorns rather more closely, I advanced a few steps. I was then wearing some dark-coloured clothes. My attendant cautioned me not to touch the thorns. The throne of the chosen prophet was sacred to the god or demon, and the sacrilegious touch of an unbeliever would awaken the wrath of offended majesty. It seemed that dark clothes were the broad gate through which the avenging demon was to enter into a man; light clothes were comparatively safe. But if the demon found an entrance, he would not be slow to take vengeance. Disease, in one of the many shapes in which it can attack mortals, would follow, and perhaps death. But the god is not hard to propitiate. A two-anna piece under his pillow, and a fowl or a young pig—presumably for sacrifice—these are all that are required. If all medical relief were so simple, what would doctors do for a living?

I was sitting lazily outside my tent one day, in another and a wilder part of the country, with a book in my hand, when a commotion among the buffaloes that had brought the tent and were tethered hard by, made me look up. I very soon found out the cause of the disturbance. It was a man carrying a bamboo over his shoulder, at one end of which was an ordinary basket and at the other was a most outlandish-looking affair. It was shaped like a box; it had peacocks' feathers stuck at the top of it, and it was decked with pieces of bright-coloured cloth, not arranged with any idea of symmetry or harmony, but simply stuck on wherever an opening presented itself. I called the man, and he brought the load. It had a small curtain in front, and this was raised in a way that brought to mind a Punch-and-Judy show in miniature. Inside, seated in the middle of another collection of tinsel and rags, of bits of silver paper and broken looking-glass, was an idol, doing its best to look terrible, but only succeeding, in my eyes, in looking intensely ridiculous. It was jet black; its eyes were bits of silver paper, promoted, perchance, from serving on mere chocolate—and holes were cut in them for the pupils. Its tongue, which was thrust out to the very furthest extent* which even a deity—and a goddess

* The goddess Kali is often represented with her tongue out. Several explanations have been given, but it is probable that it is a symbol of thirst.

too—can be expected to accomplish, was a bright vermilion and seemed to be made of sealing wax. This awful being was the goddess Komolá Bimbulá, which may be called, by way of interpretation, Mumbo Jumbo. She presides over small-pox, and travels from village to village to receive the homage which will enlist her sympathies and ensure her protection. Like a true believer, I offered my rice, whereupon her attendant priest proceeded to beat a gong violently, without any apparent object, and to intone a rigmarole which seemed to be merely Uriya names, and which was certainly nonsense. This was the incantation. After this I felt secure; small-pox had no terrors for me.

We perhaps can afford to laugh at a belief in witches and a fear of malignant deities. The goddess, whose word can bring or exclude the dreaded small-pox, or the rope hung with leaves, which is to bar the entrance of the still more awful cholera, has no interest for us save as a curiosity, or as an example of the people's superstition. Yet, is their superstition more gross than that of our servant girls, who trust to the fortune-telling of the gipsies, or sleep with wedding cake under their pillow? These people also recognize a Divine power; their conception of Him is more undefined, yet less ideal than ours; but all alike worship the Wisdom that controls the universe.

In India, as well as England, there are those who cry that they

> "Can call spirits from the vasty deep;"

and common sense always answers with Hotspur :—

> "Why, so can I, and so can any man;
> But will they come when you do call for them?"

IV.

ZEMINDARS.

Unless we except the aboriginal tribes of the hills, about whom I shall have a few words to say later, there are no more interesting figures in the Northern District of the Madras Presidency than the Uriya zemindars of Ganjam. Ranging from the position of a petty raja to one little superior to that of a wealthy and important ryot, the zemindars have yet kept to themselves a separate court and a separate *clientèle*. It is imperative on a raja to keep up at least a show of state, even if it be but the emptiest of shows, furnished out of coffers if possible more empty. Indeed, it is the necessity for state which causes so much disquietude to the Agent to the Court of Wards on assuming charge of an estate, for it is tolerably certain to be encumbered with debt, often to the extent of lakhs of rupees.

On first arriving at the palace of one of these potentates the visitor is struck by the choice which is almost invariably made of a strong position. In a district where hills are so plentiful, it is clear that there was no difficulty in obtaining a vantage ground. In no zemindari in the district is high ground wanting, and in no instance has the opportunity been neglected. That this position was chosen for purposes of defence is shown by one example, which will serve for many. "The Atagada raja's residence was secured from sudden attack by its situation between two hills. It was almost, if not entirely inaccessible, for from one hill to the other a wall of stone twenty feet high was carried to a length of about a hundred and fifty yards. The wall was pierced by a large gateway, with a square tower on each side of it." It is certain, then, that the positions of various forts were chosen for their strength, and whether considerations of art have had anything to do with this choice or no, there is no doubt that the effect, at least at a distance, is most picturesque. Surrounded on three sides by hills, for the most part densely wooded, the fort nestles half hidden, but commanding an excellent view of the plain, stretching away generally to the sea. Sometimes, however, this order of things is slightly modified, and we find the fort and the town planted in the hollow formed by a ring of hills. But whichever style obtains, the prevailing feature, that which cannot fail to strike the visitor, is always the neighbourhood of the hills. This points decisively to the uncertainty of the land tenure, to the lawlessness which must have prevailed before the occupation of the district by the British. The hills, and still more the jungles, afforded a safe retreat in case of an attack by overwhelming numbers. The chiefs preferred the paw of the wild beast to the passions of the wilder men, and by grazing their cattle in the den of the bear came near to realizing Isaiah's prophecy of the golden age. And their retreat was the more necessary because it was even less outward enemies that the chiefs had to fear than the familiar friend, who was so often ready to lift up his heel against them.

Upon a nearer approach the forts are most disappointing. The entrance gate, called the Simho Dwaro, or Lion-door, is as often as not in a dilapidated or half-repaired condition, and what should be imposing is only pitiful. Inside the gate, and on the way to the reception rooms of the zemindar, one usually passes through a confused medley of straw, old mats, tents in tatters, and other miscellaneous articles piled together to produce a confusion worse confounded. Farther on, under an open and probably temporary shed, may perhaps be seen the car, shorn of its festival splendours, and the palanquin, possibly a thing of beauty when pranked out, but now in utter and forlorn nakedness.

Things improve when we reach the zemindar. We are received with dignified courtesy, and shown into a room, small indeed, but adorned in a manner which betokens some sort of care on the part of its owner. It must be admitted that the adornments are often somewhat incongruous, and I once saw on a bracket hanging next to a picture of a blue-faced god talking to a yellow lady, two small busts of Mozart and Beethoven! One visit to a native chief is much like any other, and no description is needed here. It is to be feared, however, that the Uriya zemindar is more careful at times of himself than of his ladies. It fell within my province once to inquire of the state of the women's apartments, which are usually inferior buildings roofed with thatch. The officer replied, "Repairs are needed. The roof leaks." "Badly?" I asked. "Oh!" was the rejoinder, "a good deal. The ladies take their meals in the zenana under an umbrella to keep off the rain!"

As an organizer the Uriya zemindar, speaking

generally (for, of course, there are exceptions), cannot be held up as a shining example. The more energetic undertake the management of their own estates; but, whether from indolence or from ignorance of affairs, or, perhaps, from too nice a sense of *noblesse oblige*, the diwán is generally left in sole charge, to enrich himself as he may; and he probably does not lose the chance. Placed, as he is, with such infinite opportunities for peculation, it would be strange if he did not find some summary means of adding to the salary which he obtains from the zemindar, and which is generally utterly inadequate. He has an immense amount of patronage to bestow, and he bestows it—but not for nothing. In fact, in many cases, nearly half the estate has been given away in "inâms," or freehold grants, and on the most frivolous pretexts. For blessing the raja, for supplying goat's milk to the raja's sons, for holding a torch at the marriage ceremony —such are the frivolous and childish grounds on which acres of land are thrown away. The zemindar would no doubt consider it beneath his dignity to refuse. It is the function of a raja to be lavish.

After the diwán, the most important person is, perhaps, the gantayet or treasurer. The name itself reveals why he is important; but his counsels are also of weight in matters affecting the private policy of the zemindar. There are many other smaller officials in the palace, each bearing his separate title. Of these I may mention the tsam patnaik, or personal accountant—the word tsam denoting "presence." Many other dependants have titles conferred upon them. "The ornament," "the jewel of wisdom," and other high-flown epithets, much prized by the owners, and gained sometimes for exploits in the jungle, or for services rendered, but generally, as far as I can make out, bestowed at the whim of the zemindar. Perhaps he has a "Birthday Gazette."

The *entrée* to his presence or to his palace is given or withheld by the zemindar at his pleasure. It is a high indignity to be refused this *entrée*. In fact, the permission is rarely withheld, unless the zemindar has special cause for disliking the applicant, or reason to doubt his loyalty. On the other hand, it is a great distinction and the stamp of a gentleman (*bholo loko*) to be allowed to sit on a carpet in the presence. It would be a thankless and a tedious task to enumerate all the various degrees of distinction peculiar to a zemindar's court. But enough has been said to emphasize the point that these petty chiefs keep up a court and a state, with modes of granting honours and the reverse that find their analogies in the court even of a European sovereign.

Many and sore are the heart-burnings which the favour or anger of a zemindar arouses. It was only some few years ago that jealousies having their origin in the displeasure of the zemindar, and consequent banishment from the palace, inspired in the breast of at least one man the desire for murder, which, indeed, he all but accomplished. Palace intrigues would form the subject of a separate volume, and the limits of this essay will not allow me to treat of them. Perhaps the most famous one of recent times was that which resulted in the death by poison of the Rani of Parlakimedi. The principal actor in this was the gantayet; and this illustrates what I have remarked above, for assuredly he would have found it hard to meddle with the food given to the rani, if he had not had both influence and control in the palace.

Whatever be the character of the zemindar, viewed from a high ethical standard, there is no doubt that he is an object of the sincerest devotion to the people over whom he rules. His position towards them is somewhat analogous to that of a feudal lord, except that he has not the right to command their services in war. Right or no right, however, I do not think his people would hesitate to follow him. The maxim, "Whatever is, is right," seems to have imprinted itself forcibly on the minds of the people, and there are but few disaffected amongst them. Nevertheless, it is only in the rarer cases that the zemindar has sufficient acumen to understand that on the welfare of the people depends the prosperity of his estate. Roads are regarded only as a heavy expenditure of capital, and the opening up of new markets, and the consequent incentive to increased cultivation, is overlooked. He will allow channels and tanks to silt up rather than incur the initial outlay necessary to put them in repair and so to increase the prosperity of the people.

In the more interesting of the zemindaries the people are of a wild type, growing wilder as one approaches the hills. They are a simple folk, content with what they possess, and regard their zemindar as a being almost divine—as one whom it would be unbecoming in them to approach without the deepest reverence and humility. The traveller cannot fail to notice the difference between these people and the ryots of Government villages—too often to the disadvantage of the latter—not in prosperity, perhaps, but in character. The tribes that live at the foot of the hill have intermingled largely with the aboriginal tribes—the Khonds and the Savaras, and have inherited with their blood some of the savage, and, therefore, in one sense, simple instincts of those races. With these folk the zemindar does not deal as with the other inhabitants of the estate. They do not pay him a share of the crop, but have commuted it for an annual fixed tribute (or *nazar*), which, however, is much less than the value of the crop. This is a very small source of revenue to the raja, as they so fondly call him, for it amounts to an inconsiderable sum, and the landlord has practically no means of recovering. The contract is with the village, and it is rarely worth while to eject these men for the small satisfaction to be obtained.

Nearly every zemindari contains a large number of these hill villages, which thus swell the rent-roll of the estate without appreciably adding to its material benefit. The people live mainly on forest produce and by hunting. The moderation of zemindars in the matter of the forest is worthy of praise. The tax levied on produce is small and not burdensome; and the proximity of zemindari forests has often anything but a beneficial effect on the revenue the Government derives from this source, for the zemindar gains by underselling.

Wood—firewood and timber—honey, and the various common produce of the forests are sold by these people, and form the staple of their livelihood. Too often the large markets are remote and inaccessible for want of roads. In these cases the people flock down to the markets or local fairs, which take place in various well-known centres and at fixed times.

On such a day the simple hill-men may be seen trooping in a long line, sharing with their wives the burden of honey, of dried fruits, of, it may be, tobacco, possibly even of the gaudy beads the people are so fond of—in short, of any of those small articles, by the sale of which they hope to make a livelihood until the next fair. Here and there is a break in the line, where some well-to-do man—enriched, perhaps, by the fleecing of his more simple associates—may be seen driving his pack bullock, laden with wares of all descriptions; and those who are so fortunate as to possess the capital may even drive so many as three. The fair itself presents a curious sight. In addition to these small articles of consumption are to be found ponies, cattle, sheep, pigs, and other live stock; hides brought by Mahometans, clothes by Hindu merchants from the town; and in the centre and all around a gesticulating, shouting, jostling, screaming medley of men and women, each doing his best to out-scream the rest—and the women are invariably the victors.

But the people are essentially timid. Out of pure curiosity I went into the fair to see what was going on. The unwonted sight of a European struck terror into the hearts of the vendors, and, leaving their wares, they fled helter-skelter, in spite of the blandest smiles and the most reassuring words!

But apart from these more peaceful avocations the people are much devoted to hunting; and this for two reasons. It affords an excellent pastime; the excitement of the chase is as meat and drink to them, and the results of it often go to form their dinner. On many estates the zemindars keep a special staff of trained servants, shikaris, whose business it is to find him game, and to provide and arrange for the sport, somewhat as gamekeepers do in England. These shikaris, though, often go out on their own account. The weapons they carry are of a curious and varied type. A few of them may carry antiquated matchlocks of the European pattern; but the more characteristic weapons are the Uriya gun, the bows and arrows, and the *tangi* or axe. The gun is of immense length, and is bound somewhat after the manner of a gigantic flute, with curious bindings of steel or silver. It is often five or six feet long, and is, in consequence, very heavy and unwieldy. The bows and arrows are (save for the feathers and the iron tip) made entirely out of bamboo, the bow being made of the wood, and the string of the bark—and very tough they are. The arrows have sometimes a head of blunt wood, for the purpose of stunning the animal, in place of the usual sharp iron head. With these arrows the people will attack and kill even panthers, though this is probably rather dangerous sport. The *tangi* is familiar to all who know Ganjam, and it is the most characteristic weapon in the district. It is a sort of battle-axe, often ornamented with wire bound round the pole; the head, too, is fashioned into various shapes, according to the use to which the weapon is to be put. For the most part, however, *tangis* in the plains are simple axes used for cutting wood. They are poor weapons at close quarters with a tiger or a bear.

They have one curious mode of shikar, which,

however, I have never been fortunate enough to see. Having chosen a secure place, they dig a hole, in which they take up their position. A few yards away a fire is lighted, while the man in the pit rattles some instrument or plays on the tom-tom. It is said that the animals are attracted by the light and by the sound, and so fall an easy prey. I give this for what it is worth. Credat Judaeus Apella! Which being interpreted means, "I would rather see it done first!"

Many of the zemindars have done a great deal of big game shooting, and some can show a really fine score of panthers and even of tigers to their credit. Besides these, the sport they most affect is deer shooting. Bears, I believe, fall under the protection of the Hindu religion, and it is comparatively rarely that these animals are molested. I am sorry to say that the zemindars do not always show such nice discrimination. I have known one shoot trapped hares, and I have heard another fire at a jackal!

One more point remains to be noticed—

Just as the Acts of the English Parliament are dated, not by the year of the Christian era, but by the year of the reigning sovereign, so the people of these zemindaris often use, not the year of the

Hindu cycle, or the Mahometan era, but the year of the reigning Raja of Puri; and the method of reckoning this year is so curious that it deserves to be described in detail.

The first year of the reign is called, not one, but "la'bho" or "gain." The counting then proceeds in the ordinary course, but, with the exception of the figure 10, all figures ending with 7 or 0 are omitted. This is called the "onko." Thus, if a raja has reigned 21½ years he would be said to be in the twenty-fifth "onko," 7, 17, and 20 being omitted. The idea is, I suppose, capable of explanation, but the inclusion of 10 prevents any theory being formed by induction. I have never found any explanation for it myself, and the only practical result is that it is very confusing.

Now the rest of the acts of the zemindars, and the court that they keep, and the wars and rebellions they have made against the Government, are they not written in the book of the "District Manual"?

V.

KHONDS AND SAVARAS.

THE Khonds and Savaras of Ganjam district are so intimate with the Uriyas, and have adopted in so many cases their manners, customs, and language, that, though the subject lies somewhat outside the scope of this present essay, a few words by way of appendix will not be out of place.

Of the Khonds proper, this is, however, not the place to speak. They, lying in the arms of their mountains, have but little intercourse with the Uriyas of the plain. They are girt about on all sides with natural ramparts, and their abode is only accessible by passes, which offer few inducements to the traveller, and no facilities to the trader.

Khonds there are, however, who inhabit a small range of hills within five miles of Berhampore, the chief town of the district. Here they live in seclusion and in freedom, but also in the lowest depths of

II

squalor and poverty. Khonds they are indeed in name—

> "Sed quantum mutatus ab illo
> Hectore, qui redit exuvias indutus."

Exuviae! They are lucky if they have one garment, and that such as they can call their own! Once they loved gay colours. True Khond dresses, both male and female, are full of stripes and patterns in blue, yellow, and red. Where has gone the love of colour? Instead of the long waistcloth ending in tails of blue and red, the man binds about him a wretched rag that can hardly be called a garment. Colour there is none, if we except that colour which a once white cloth takes on for want of water and washing. Once the women took a delight in decking themselves with flowers, and a pride in the silver ornaments that jangled on their naked breasts. Where are now the grasses that adorned them, and the innocence that allowed them to go clothed only from the waist? Gone! withered by the blast of the breath of a "superior civilization." Alas for the poor Khond! Like his brethren, he, too, is girt about with hills; he, too, is placed in the midst of solitude. For the hills themselves are left entirely to the Khond. The slopes are crowned with dense bamboo forest and fruit trees, all preserved by the Government. Here the Khond might have been secure, but the wall of Paradise was not high enough, and Satan entered in the shape of the Uriya money-lender.

> "Due entrance he disdained;
> At one slight bound high overleaped all bound."

The money-lenders have sucked the life out of the unfortunate Khond. His lands are mortgaged; his trees are mortgaged; and besides his land and his trees he has nothing. In 1884 the Forest Department took up three blocks in the Mohiri hills, comprising all the hill slopes. This was a death-blow to the Khond. At one stroke was taken from him the power of cultivating the land in his own national way—the only way he really understands. For this cultivation the dense undergrowth is cut down and burnt, and the ashes are allowed to lie on the land as manure. On the land thus prepared he sows broadcast the crop—it may be of cholum, or of some coarse millet. The seed is cast on stony ground, where there is not much depth of earth, and the scanty crop forces its head through the crevices of the stones. Such a mode of cultivation is, of course, beyond all measure extravagant. The land which is sown one year must be allowed to lie fallow until the jungle has grown up again sufficiently dense to justify another burning and another sowing. Such as it is, however, it is the Khond's darling pursuit. The slopes of the hills alone were covered with thick jungle, and when these were appropriated there was nothing left.

The lands he had mortgaged now became a serious consideration. It was clear that, so long as he could support himself by the roving system of cultivation, the lands lying in the valley were of little use to him; the mortgagee could till the land if he liked. Now, however, he was thrown back upon this land for his subsistence, and part—often the greater part—of the produce was swallowed up in payment of the usurious interest on the debts with which he was burdened. Nor was this all. By reserving the forests, the Government also reserved the fruit trees, which formerly the Khond had been privileged to enjoy. The trees were leased to the highest bidder and the fruit sold by him. Thus was their second means of livelihood cut off or, at any rate, diminished. The Government, however, has recently made large concessions to the Khonds in the matter of these fruit trees, and a great cause of discontent has thus been removed.

With the forests and the fruit trees the Khonds have also lost the right or privilege of hunting the wild animals in the jungles. This is probably no great hardship. The Khonds do not seem to look upon hunting as a means of obtaining food. Indeed, it would be difficult to class them among the earlier stages of civilization. They are certainly not nomadic or pastoral. Agriculturists they may be called, but their agriculture is of a kind known only to themselves and to one or two other aboriginal tribes. Hunters they are not, though they are fond of the sport for its own sake, and though each man has his bows and arrows made all of bamboo. Yet here again we are forced to cry "Ichabod! the glory is departed." Gone are the hairpins of sambur bone—an inestimable treasure in the eyes of the true hill Khond. Gone are the floral decorations and the fantastic head-dresses, which are the pride of the mountain tribes. In dull, unromantic squalor our Khond lives, moves, and has his being; and ever as he moves is heard the clanking upon his wrists of the fetters of his debt. Yet for all this he is happy. He is not free from the land tax; his neck is under the yoke of the Forest Department. But he is happy. He clears the jungle by foul means, if fair will not serve, and carries on a surreptitious cultivation. I ought rather to say "his defiant cultivation," for the patches upon the hills are perfectly conspicuous; but who is going to climb three thousand feet to find the nest empty and the bird flown? He steals the firewood from the forest, and probably filches the fruit. He is happy, because his wants are few; he is happy in that he lives for to-day; he is happy, because it is his nature to be happy. His ignorance is bliss to him, and he counts it folly to be wise.

In thus presenting an outline sketch of this isolated body of Khonds, I have not been able to describe any manners and customs peculiar to the tribe. Living, as they do, surrounded by Uriya villages, brought into contact with the Uriyas in all the affairs of every-day life, the Khond of the hills has lost his own peculiar customs and traditions, and has, in a large measure, assimilated himself to the predominating Uriyas. In features alone he is essentially a Khond. The purity of stock is maintained by the restrictions of caste. In respect of his customs he is at a disadvantage, compared with the Savara, if disadvantage it be to relinquish national customs in favour of those of a higher civilization.

It is of the Savara and his home on the slopes of Mahendragiri, the highest hill in the district, that I intend to add a few notes.

If the people are happy who have no history, then assuredly the Savaras, whose dwelling is in these high hills, are the happiest people in the world. Above them the hill, below them the hill, on either side the hill, unmolested by the so-called civilization of the plain, unhampered by the officiousness of village servants, the Savaras live a life of steady monotony—going forth to their labour in the morning, and returning to their rest at night. The Savara's world is around him; he knows nothing of courts of justice or forest laws; he has never heard of railways or canals. His dominion is the mountain—the mountain is his all. It gives him firewood, it gives him water; out of it he gets his scanty crops, roaming year by year from place to place, and burning down the jungle as he goes, after the manner lately described. The only thing the hill does not give him is clothes, and of these he has such a scanty stock that they need not be included among the necessaries of life. His little village of perhaps ten houses is built on the side of the hill, upon a small plateau levelled for the purpose. The view from it is magnificent; the situation is well chosen. For the view, probably, the Savara cares little; the situation he has deliberately selected. But for all that from November to June he has the advantage of us, he must be very uncomfortable in the rains.

"The conies are but a feeble folk, yet make they their houses in the rocks," are the words of Agur, the son of Jakeh. Of all the aboriginal tribes of the presidency, the Savaras are perhaps of the least account. The Khonds, famous for the human "Meriah" sacrifice, from time to time demonstrate their existence by the murder of a policeman or by a little rising on their own account. Like the spider, which is in kings' palaces, the Toda encamps about the Queen of the Hills. But the Savaras are but a feeble folk, dwelling among the rocks—not perhaps pre-eminent for wisdom, though in one or two respects they set an example which their more civilized brethren need not be ashamed to follow.

The house of a Savara is a tiny hut, with but one small room. Here are his few possessions—a cooking pot or two; perhaps a bow and arrows; a few skins of the hill-squirrel for festival purposes. Sometimes outside, in a tiny pen attached to the house, is the pig or a few fowls. In the small hut are gathered father, mother, and perhaps four or five children. Here they lie down to sleep at night, adults and children, male and female, without distinction or difference. Under such conditions it is impossible that husband and wife should enjoy the pleasures of the conjugal relation. "It is their custom i' th' afternoon to sleep." They retire into the jungle to rest, and the gate of Paradise is guarded by a flaming sword that turns every way. For across the path which leads into Eden is laid a bough or a bramble to warn the profane intruder. The sign is always respected, and the inmates are as secure as though they were guarded by a veritable angel with his sword of fire.

In a life of such simplicity it is hard to discover manners and customs which are worth our notice; but the Savaras, like other nations and tribes, are peculiar in the manner of their marriages and of their funerals.

The first step on the road to the altar is to ask the hand of the maiden in marriage. To this end the bridegroom and his father take in their hands an arrow and a pot of liquor, and go to seek the girl. Arrived at her parents' house, they strike the arrow into the lintel, where it remains fixed, and then deposit the liquor in the street; or, perhaps, it would be more accurate to say outside the house, seeing that Savara villages do not usually boast of streets. So far all is dumb show. The hint has been given, and it is for the girl's father to take it. As the houses are generally open, and as probably the suitor contrives to make a good deal of noise in fixing the arrow, there is little chance of such visitors not being observed within doors. The father of the girl has perhaps fixed upon another beau; or he has taken a dislike to the suitor; or the blood of the haughty Savara De Veres runs in his veins, and he will not consent to a marriage which he considers beneath him. In such cases he will come out of the house, and with a curt "Begone, you and your liquor," expressed more or less politely, he will dismiss both the suitor and the suit. The disappointed swain carries away the arrow and the liquor, to search for the hand of a maiden more complaisant, and to touch the heart of a less obdurate father-in-law.

If, on the other hand, the fair Belinda's sire be in an amiable mood, or if the match be generally desirable, the father will come out of the house and carry back the pot of liquor. The village is then invited —not many guests will appear, one may suppose, when the village consists of five or six houses. All drink the liquor. This is the ratification of the clan, and the betrothal is complete. The bridegroom elect goes off with his father, and a few days afterwards returns, this time with more substantial offerings—goats, pigs, and fowls, as well as, of course, the inevitable liquor. Then another feast, with plenty of good cheer and more noise—and bride and bridegroom go off, to live, we will hope, happily ever afterwards.

Such is the custom when the ceremony is performed, as one may say, "with full choral service;" when the contracting parties are the Howards or the Seymours of the Savara nation. But a marriage in low life is less gorgeous, though more practical, and shows a foresight with which one would not credit so uncivilized a race. The girl is simply demanded in marriage, and if her father agrees to the contract, he and the bridegroom elect go into partnership, and cultivate for two or three years. Though the marriage expenses will not amount to more than ten rupees, one can imagine that it would take some years to amass even that, since the cultivation is merely burning the jungle and sowing the seed broadcast. Even after two or three years of probation and prudence, it will sometimes happen that there is not enough money for the wedding; but the Savara of the hills does not often get seriously into debt. The marriage feast goes on in the manner already described, though probably on a smaller scale.

In the manner of his funerals the Savara is evidently a disciple of the utilitarian school. The dead man's hands and feet are tied together, and a bamboo is passed through them. Two men then carry the corpse, slung in this fashion, to the burning-ground. Many of my readers may have seen, and seen with indignation, a pig slung on a pole in a similar way.

When the burning-ground is reached, two posts are stuck up, and the bamboo, with the corpse tied to it, is placed crosswise on the posts, so that the structure looks like a Rugby football goal-post in miniature, though the idea is really more analogous to that of the kettle in a gipsy encampment. Then below the corpse a fire is lighted, and there begins a fizzling, and a hissing, and a spluttering, until the ropes which are tied round the hands and feet give way. Down falls the corpse; up leap the flames, and that which was, is not.

Two small points in their strange burial service remain to be noticed. For the fire, the Savara always uses the wood of the mango tree. It is difficult to say why this should be. It is said that the Savara does not care for mangoes, but this is not a sufficient reason for the exclusive use of this wood in cremation. The Savara man is always burnt in the portion of ground—one cannot call it a field—which he last cultivated. We all know how much store is set by burial in consecrated ground, and it is probable that the custom has originated in an analogous feeling.

The cultivation of the hills is the Savara's be-all in life and his end-all after death. His last resting-place is that ground on which he has toiled from day to day, from which he drew his daily sustenance. The whole ceremony is so ludicrously practical, that it needs such a touch of sentiment for its salvation. And yet when the poor Savara is thus consigned to his own grand native hills, one may fitly sing over him the requiem—

> "In the vast cathedral leave him;
> God accept him, Christ receive him."

And what of the country which the Savaras inhabit? A long chain of hills runs up from the Vizagapatam district along the west of Ganjam, until they become merged in the Eastern Ghâts, and the Savaras are lost in the abodes of the Khonds. In the southern part of our district there is a regular succession of forts, each governed by an Uriya chief called the "Bissoyi." Of them and of their wars with the British I shall not speak here. Wars, and burnings, and executions, are matters of history proper, and can be read in the annals of the times. The heads of the Savara clans are called "Gomango" and "Mondolo," and much prized are the titles, though the Uriya invaders took from them the exercise of real authority.

The most conspicuous of the Savara hills is called Mahendragiri, and round its venerable head cluster many legends. The hill is something under 5000 feet in height, and near the top, upon a small plateau, stands a rest-house, the property of a courteous zemindar. Here is an ideal retreat for the seeker after solitude. Far away lies the sea, more than twenty miles as the crow flies. Underneath the hills—great rugged mountains looked at from below—stretch out on either hand, tumbled and in disorder, like some giant children resting after their game of play, while from above, the parent Manendra looks down upon and watches over them. In the distance paddy fields and pastures are unrolled to the sea-shore, while here and there shining strips show where the tanks are dotted over the face of the country. Immediately below, trees lie in the lap of a lower spur—bright green, red, yellow, and olive, all mingled together. In front issues the smoke and crackle of a great furnace, where some Savara has, seemingly for pure wantonness, set the jungle in a blaze. It is curious to feel oneself so far above the dwellings of men, to hear no sound but the twittering of the birds in the wood, and the sigh of the wind in the trees. For ordinarily the Savara does not cultivate the higher slopes, and the rest-house is a thousand feet above even the least of those small clusters of houses called by courtesy villages. Above you an owl hoots; below perhaps you will hear the strange, harsh cry of the jungle sheep or the sambur, but for the most part all is silent, for the hill is very destitute of animal life.

Immediately behind the rest-house there is a small open plateau sloping gently up to the final ascent of tumbled rocks and boulders. All around are scattered temples—miniature huts, from which the god has long since departed—huts made of rough stone, and innocent of plaster or mortar. Among them rises a more imposing structure, dedicated to the god Jejushti, well put together, and adorned with a fluted pattern carved in the stone. The shape is the ordinary Uriya barrel, which I have described before. But the stones of which the temple is built are of enormous size. The whole is symmetrical, and shows a considerable progress in the art of architecture. Right on the top of the hill is another temple, dedicated to the god Bhimo: this is made of magnificent boulders, piled one above the other. The roof is a simple, solid square of rock, and upon this is another enormous stone, also a single block, shaped into circular form and fluted at the edges. Upon this rests the crown of the temple. The weight of these stones is so enormous that the walls of the temple are in many parts crushed out of their places, and gaps are everywhere to be seen. In one or two cases the weight of the vast mass has, as it were, hewn off gigantic chips weighing several tons, and these are lying now around the temple. From a rough measurement which I made, I calculated that the roof stone weighs over 150 tons! Such were the bricks which were used by the giants of those days.

Tradition says that these two temples were built by two brothers, divine or semi-divine, who had originally lived together in harmony on the top of the mountain and received conjointly the prayers and the offerings of the hill tribes. But discord arose between them, and the one, Jejushti, built for himself the temple near which the rest-house now stands, while the other, Bhimo, not to be outdone, erected his shrine on the extreme summit of the hill, outvying his brother both in elevation of site and in grandeur of execution. Each invited the people to come and worship his sole divinity—and here the legend ends. Which was victorious, whether they afterwards were reconciled, we do not know. Only the temples stand there, memorials of the divine power, as the walls of Laomedon owned the magic of Apollo's lyre and the skill of Poseidon's hands.

Such is the legend; but what a field for speculation is opened up! For besides the two completed temples are scattered all round huge blocks of stone, with edges squared and faces hewn, the materials for other temples. Perchance a king who oppressed his people sought to win heaven by building temples, and gained a doubtful virtue by an intolerable tyranny; but another exodus scattered his plans to the winds. Or a strong and prosperous king bequeathed to his son the task of completing the coronation of Mahendra. But the son was a weak prince; the kingdom was torn by dissensions, and the work remained unfinished. Or again seven years of famine succeeded to seven years of plenty; Pharaoh's lean kine had eaten up Pharaoh's fat kine, and labour was there none. Or perhaps the pious king died, and the impious son paid no tribute to the gods of his father. But to what end is speculation? There lie the stones, their history locked within that secret drawer; and who shall unlock it?

There is yet another legend connected with the hill. Half-way down, in the steepest part of the steepest ghât, is a stone image, roughly hewn into some semblance of a female figure. This is the Old Woman of the Mountain. The story goes that as she was toiling down the hill, in far-off times, "before the sun shone and the moon gave her light" (as a Savara expressed it to me), her foot slipped, and she rolled down the precipice. The fall killed her at once, and she burst asunder in the midst. The pious men of the mountain have put up this image in the way, that travellers may worship, and are so faithful to their tradition that they have divided the image "close to the waist." It is hard to destroy the romance, and to ask the practical question, whether the legend is not rather the effect than the cause of the broken image.

Here we will leave the Savaras and their hills and their legends. Their wants are few; their life is simple, and they are dominated by the superior civilization of the Uriyas in the plains. But they are yet free—free as long as their mountain home remains to them. Mahendragiri is the outlying rampart. Behind, across a valley into which one looks down a sheer two thousand feet, rises Singaráj, the lion king, and all his subject hills, ranging line after line behind him. The mountain looks like some monarch, who, leading his well-ordered regiments against the foe, had met with another Perseus and another Gorgon's head. And there they stand, arrested, petrified, their king at their head—immovable battalions for evermore.

A FORGOTTEN REBELLION

In the south of the district of Ganjam, some four and twenty miles from the railway, there lies, in the pleasant valley of the Vamsadhára, the little town of Parlakimedi. Placed for many years under the direct control of the Government, and of late ruled over by an enlightened prince and a prudent manager, the country has proved to be the garden of the district. Flanked by a range of hills known as the "Maliahs," irrigated by river channels, its cultivated fields varied continually by thickly wooded hills, the country thrives, even while its less fortunate neighbours are in distress. The ryots live in peace and security. The crops are gathered, the rents are paid, and all goes "merry as a marriage bell."

The town itself has few attractions of any sort, and none of name. Its traditions and its history are purely native. No Francis Xavier spent his life here; no apostles from the setting sun have left traditions; no western companies have risen to fame or sunk into oblivion here. Perhaps its interest is that its history is purely native. At a time when the influence of western nations was making itself felt all over India —when Bentinck was abolishing widow-burning and organized murder; when Lutheran missionaries were disputing with the learned Brahmins of Tanjore, and Catholics were converting the fishermen of Tinnevelly—the picture of the Uriya chiefs revelling in unbridled lawlessness, is interesting from its very contrast. The scene is barbaric. Some of the episodes are worthy of Attila or Brennus. To a barbarian scene belong barbarous words, strange names of men and places, paiks and sanads and Bissoyis, not understanded of the multitude.

The places which belong to this particular page of Indian history have all disappeared. The Four Streets are no longer to be found. The palace, where so many combinations were formed, only to be shaken in the march of events into new ones, like the colours of the kaleidoscope—all these have given place to a new palace, built from an European design, and fronting the main street. At the other end of the street stands a flourishing college. Printing and the arts are encouraged, and—last wonder of a civilizing age! —a newspaper has recently made its appearance.

Such is the Parlakimedi of to-day. Far different

was its aspect a century ago. The town was then the scene of rapine and riot, and not seldom of bloodshed. Everywhere smoke rose from the burning villages; crops were destroyed, women outraged; men were sent into the jungles, shorn of ears or nose, to seek from the gentler tigers the mercy denied to them by their fellow-men. All was insecurity and war, where now there reign security and peace. War, too, of a barbarous type, not governed by treaties of St. Petersburg or Geneva conventions; war, where one party at least harried the innocent people, as an incentive to battle, and ravaged the fields out of sheer wantonness.

In 1798 the zemindar, by refusing to submit to authority, and by neglecting to pay his tribute, forced the Government to adopt strong measures. He was therefore confined; his son, Purnshottama Narayana Deo, and his nephew, Durga Raj, were at the same time secured and were sent to Masulipatam, on the east coast. These things were the beginning of sorrows. The people—at least those who espoused the cause of the zemindar—rose in arms. They seized villages, they carried off the grain, they put a stop to all collection of revenue by threatening the peasants. On all sides appeared blackened ruins of hamlets, on all sides men fled to the hills and the jungles to escape the wrath of the insurgents.

The Government at first tried concession. Purnshottama Deo and Durga Raj were brought back to the district from Masulipatam. The effect was magical. The power of the insurgents did not merely dwindle, it vanished; their forces were not merely weakened, they melted away. The country, though desolated, was again at peace, and all that remained to be done was to provide for its administration. The estate which had been forfeited by the late zemindar was now conferred on Purnshottama Deo and the management was entrusted to Durga Raj.

For thirteen years all went well. The zemindar died, and was succeeded by a minor son. Durga Raj was ruler and manager in word and in deed; but in 1813 he died, and the old fires of insurrection burst out afresh. This time they were fanned by the intrigues of the ladies of the palace; and for nineteen years the country was thrown into confusion to satisfy an old woman's lust of power and a young woman's caprice or vanity.

The immediate cause of revolt was the appointment of a new manager, Padmanabha Deo. It was supposed that this man, who was the son of Durga

Raj, would be respected by all; but, for some reason, he seems to have been obnoxious from the first. It is now that the Bissoyis appear on the scene, and it is necessary to relate who and what they were.

As has already been said, Parlakimedi is flanked by a range of hills known as the Maliahs. In these hills are a number of forts, in which the Bissoyis or hill chieftains reside. Each of them holds a small court of his own; each has his armed retainers and his executive staff. They were set to rule over the hill tracts, to curb the lawlessness of the aboriginal tribes of the mountains—the Khonds and the Savaras. They were, in fact, lords of the marches, and were in a measure independent, but they appear to have been under the suzerainty of the raja at Kimedi, and they were also generally responsible to Government. Such men were valuable friends, and dangerous enemies. Their influence amongst their own men was complete; their knowledge of their own country was perfect. It was they, and they only, who could thread their way through the tangled and well-nigh impenetrable jungle by footpaths known only to themselves. Hence, when they became enemies, they could entrench themselves in positions which were almost impregnable. Now a road leads to every fort; the jungles have disappeared; the Bissoyis still have armed retainers, and still keep a measure of respect; but their power to sting is gone, and the officer of Government goes round every year on the peaceful, if prosaic, occupation of examining schools and inspecting vaccination.

Such were the men who at this crisis induced the widow of the late zemindar, Gajapati Pata Mahadevi, to rebel. Once more the smoke arose from the burning villages; once more the peasants were harried, and the crops were plundered. A force was sent against the rebels, but the difficulties were too great, and it was obliged to retire. Negotiation was then tried, and a complete inquiry into the complaints was offered. In 1814 a memorable interview took place between the Collector of the district and the Bissoyis. Great preparations were made, and at the appointed time a band of Savaras, armed with bows and arrows, marched to the camp; but no one followed! The Bissoyis, fearing the treachery of which they knew themselves capable, had gathered in a grove at some distance. Hour after hour passed, and they gave no sign. At length they arrived, escorted by a thousand to twelve hundred men, armed with matchlocks and bows and arrows! The conference showed symptoms of becoming turbulent. It was settled, however, that the chiefs should present their grievances in writing. But this came to nothing, and three days afterwards another meeting was held. The one cry was for the removal of Padmanabha Deo. It was vain to ask, "What evil hath he done?" The people could not brook minute inquiries into detached points; they could not understand the sifting of evidence. The clouds grew blacker, and a storm was brewing. We may imagine the feelings of the Collector and his assistant when they felt themselves practically alone with these chiefs, who could command a thousand men at a moment's notice! The Jeringhi Bissoyi turned to the Guma Bissoyi and said, "Are not the golden sparrows flown into our cage? Let us watch them, till we get what we want." Luckily they were dissuaded by one of the Collector's clerks, and the Englishmen were delivered. In the end the manager was removed, and the country was again restored to tranquillity.

The fire was suppressed, but not put out, and in 1816 it was again fanned to a flame by the former manager, Padmanabha Deo. It was, however, in 1817 that matters were really brought to a crisis. In that year the head English clerk of the Collector's office was appointed to be manager. He was a Tamil, his name Subaraya Mudali. What must have been the consternation, and even terror of this poor man, when he found himself tossed neck and heels into the midst of a den of roaring lions, for so the wild Bissoyis and the insurgent Uriyas must have seemed to him! With what relief must he have received the news of his removal, which came a few months later!

Meanwhile the political parties had taken definite form. On the one side was the Pata Maha Devi, elder widow of the late zemindar, supported by the Bissoyi of Guma; on the other the younger widow, whose chief adherent was the Bissoyi of Jeringhi. The authorities felt themselves obliged to play a waiting game, though their eyes were open and they expected the worst. "The violent struggle for power," says a report of that year, "attended by the usual disturbances," rapine, outrage, and destruction, "may be expected in a year or two." The authorities felt their weakness; the turbulent semi-military hordes knew their power. On the one hand, they could afford to laugh at the empty threats of troops which never came, or, if they came, were harmless; on the other, they were filling their pockets with unlawful gain.

So things went on from bad to worse for the next thirteen years. The plunderings and burnings continued—not, of course, all the time, but with too brief intervals of peace. At times a startling episode stands out in greater prominence. In 1822 the town rose and drove out the raja's diwán, or chief minister, and the revolting spectacle of the heads of five murdered Savaras, exposed on the walls after the manner of our forefathers, shocked the European humanity of the civil officers. In 1827 the two rival queens joined their forces against the raja's wife. They were driven out, and fled, while their favourite was thrown into a well near the palace. Manager after manager only added fuel to the fire. The real masters of the country were the "town peons," the peons of the Four Streets. These men, who, during this period, degenerated into a compound of bully and savage, were the household troops of the zemindar; they collected his revenues and guarded his borders. At this time they were indispensable to any party, and they did that which was right in their own eyes. They plundered the treasury, they pillaged the country, they drove away the managers, and set up the idol of their fleeting fancy, to knock it down again when the mood passed.

In 1831 a gentleman of the name of Eden was appointed to the district. From the report of Mr. Russell, who rather damns him with faint praise, he seems to have been a quiet, peace-loving man, afraid of responsibility, and averse to strong measures, though he once showed himself fearless enough in a critical position. He went to Parlakimedi with some sepoys, but, finding his approach was resisted on the way, he determined to go on alone. Meanwhile the insurgents opposed the soldiery, seized the baggage, captured a company of sixty men, and cut off the communications. Masters of the situation, they could dictate their own terms; they were bought off with a present of 19,000 rupees, and once more peace was restored.

This was in August, 1831. In September of the same year the storm broke out afresh. In May the Government had taken what seems to the reader of to-day a very extraordinary step. They had restored the hated Padmanabha Deo, upon whose removal the Bissoyis of 1816 had insisted with such determination. Nor was the experiment more successful now. All parties in the State agreed to reconcile their differences, and to unite for the expulsion of the object of their common hatred. At the same time it is very doubtful if any measure short of war would have been successful. The insurgents loved anarchy for its own sake. The so-called grievances were but a pretext; they found they could get gold for the gathering, and there was no man to take it from them. However this may be, the death of Padmanabha Deo, which soon followed, produced quiet. The parties, who were united by the common bond of hatred to him, now began again to look each after its own interests.

At this juncture Mr. Russell arrived in Ganjam, with a special commission from the Government of Fort St. George. His first care was to try and find out who were the instigators of rebellion, and the universal cry of the people laid the guilt on the heads of Rakana Chendrudu, the Sirdar of the town peons, and Gopinadha Patnaik, the chief Uriya accountant. These men had already, in 1823, been put upon their trial for riot, robbery, and arson, but the Court of Faujdari Adalut, distrusting the evidence, acquitted them. In 1827 the same men were found to be fomenting the disturbances and directing the intrigues; and they were therefore banished from the zemindari. The authorities, however, seem to have been hoodwinked, and they were allowed to return upon their protesting fidelity. This was a sham. In 1831 the same two men, though pretending to side with the manager, were in secret league with the rebels, and paralyzed all the schemes of the party to which they professed to belong. It is difficult to understand how the authorities were persuaded into letting them return ; but it is easy to be wise after the event. The town peons were all-powerful, and these men had unbounded influence over them. It may have been policy, therefore, to tolerate them, and at least to affect to trust them. The event proved it was mistaken policy. Taken three times from the zemindari, and three times restored, they seemed, both to the town peons and to the people, to bear charmed lives. The town peons obeyed with alacrity the congenial orders to plunder and destroy ; the people suffered and were dumb.

When Mr. Russell arrived these men sent him submissive letters : not that they wrote them themselves, they were too clever for that. The letters were supposed to come from the Bissoyis, but Mr. Russell was not asleep. He managed to get hold of an Uriya called Dasu Patnaik, and this was no mean acquisition, for such was the terror of the inhabitants, that many wealthy men came, like Nicodemus, by night, for fear of the town peons and their adherents. Dasu Patnaik managed to get two very curious letters for Mr. Russell—letters which speak of outrage in the most open and indifferent way, which chuckle over treachery, and mix up the common affairs of life with plans for resistance and wholesale destruction. The letters both came from Rakana Chendrudu, and were written in 1818 and 1832. "If you plunder four villages and the Fair," he says in one of them, "it will be well. . . The Bissoyis of seven forts came there, and the Jeringhi Bissoyi pledged himself by an oath to the Mudali (the then manager) that he would get in the collections, *after which* they laid in wait on the road, wounded his sayer peon, and robbed him of his seal, his badge and the money he was carrying." And again in the letter of 1832: "Collect the people and the peons of the Four Streets, and stockade the pass. *I will come with Padmanabha Deo,*" whose ally he professed himself to be. "Then let Jaggili Bissoyi take the peons and burn some villages. If you do this, I will prevent the troops from going westward. You wrote for beaten rice. There is none to be got here. You can get it at Gunupur." There is a charming candour about these letters. Innocent remarks about household necessaries are dovetailed into schemes for betraying troops and burning villages; but more remarkable still is the insolence, exulting in shameless treachery, which is contained in the "after which" of the first letter.

Mr. Russell was not the man to let the grass grow under his feet. He determined to capture these two men, and one "Godeyapaud" (for so the name is written in the report). Troops were collected; a panic seized the rebels, and Gopinádha Patnaik and the Sirdar were easily taken. The attempt to capture Godeyapaud failed. A night attack was made upon his house, and was very nearly successful. He had closed the approach with bushes, and a slight noise was made in pulling them out of the way. His ears, sharp as those of a wild animal, warned him to fly at once, and he obeyed the warning. His wife and children, however, were captured.

He fled to Gumá, and the Bissani, the mother of the young Bissoyi, refused to deliver him up. Martial law was then declared, and, the people of Gumá being now openly at war, conflicts took place frequently and with varying success. The fruits of victory, however, remained with the Government. The troops, though they had done little, had at least penetrated to places hitherto deemed inaccessible.

The ringleaders of the revolt were prisoners. A rude blow had been dealt at the fancied security of the insurgents, and the people, recovering their confidence, began to come back to their deserted villages.

At this stage light is thrown upon a curious point of the criminal law of that day. The two prisoners were tried by the court of Faujdari Adalut, and were of course found guilty of rebellion and treason. Every one looked for their execution, but the highest punishment which the law allowed was transportation for life. Mr. Russell very naturally expresses his surprise. If there is one crime more than another for which death seems the only fitting penalty, that crime is treason. If there is one crime more than another for which the sentence of death has been established by precedent, at any rate for Englishmen, that crime is treason. Page after page of English history contains the names of dukes, earls, marquises, gentlemen, queens, nay, even one king—who were executed for this offence. Nor was the case of the two rebels a technical case of treason. Rebellion had been fostered for its own sake; law and order had been resisted, because the rebels profited by anarchy. It is strange that the law which executed Nanda

Kumar for forgery had no power over the lives of traitors.

When the news was known, that these men were not to die, the effect was disastrous. The people had seen them thrice removed and thrice restored. They bore charmed lives, and nothing short of death would break the spell. In some vague, mysterious way their influence would stretch over sea from the place of exile, to work a renewal of miseries to the country.

Such was the consternation, that martial law, which had till now been confined to Gumá, was now proclaimed throughout the state. Negotiations were also opened with the Bissoyi of Jeringhi and the Bissani of Gumá for the delivery of the rebel, Godeyapaud. The interpreter was one Dasarathi Jenna, leader of the town peons. Mr. Russell trusted neither this man nor the Bissoyi, and events showed that he was right; but for the time it was necessary to dissemble. Unfortunately Mr. Russell had to leave the district for a while. No sooner had he gone than disaster followed.

The Bissoyi had fixed the date and place where he had to deliver up the rebel, but, like a true Oriental, he kept on making excuses for delay. The troops were then commanded by a Major

Baxter, who, intending to bring matters to a crisis, resolved to go in person to the Bissoyi's fort. His zeal seems to have carried him to the borders of rashness. He set out with a body of troops, sending a havildar in advance to reconnoitre. The havildar found the road blocked with trees, and sent back word. Major Baxter, with that false sense of security which at times seems so strangely to take possession of expeditions of this kind, took no notice. The men marched on without loading, totally unsuspicious of an ambush, when suddenly, on turning a corner, they were fired upon. Major Baxter was wounded in the arm, and the havildar in the knee. Some of the men probably received wounds also, but the party managed to fight its way back. Major Baxter died of his wound, and the havildar lost his leg.

Mr. Russell returned in November, 1833, only to find things worse than ever. The Bissoyis had again made war upon the defenceless ryots, and fire and rapine were as busy as ever. Several conflicts had taken place between the troops and the rebels. Above all, how was the Bissoyi of Jeringhi to be treated? The Bissoyi had written to Major Baxter, asking him not to come to Jeringhi, and objecting to the presence of the troops. He had in a manner hinted that an advance in force would be considered a declaration of war, and in this he seems to have been little to blame. But afterwards he plundered the villages, attacked the troops, and shut the passes; and he had thus shown himself to be in open rebellion. It was impossible to receive him again upon the old footing: it was impossible to pardon him, so long, at least, as no overtures came from him. Meanwhile it was necessary to temporize for other reasons. The crops were ripe for harvest. The dew at that season of the year is very heavy in Ganjam, and exposure would be certain to bring on fever. The troops had no artillery. Lastly, Mr. Russell hoped that, if he ceased from open hostility, the enemy would refrain from violence. But it was necessary to keep open a certain pass; and a party, which was sent to occupy it, was fired upon, and had to retire with loss. All hopes of peace were at an end. War was the only course left.

Faction, which plays so important a part in the politics of Indian villages and Indian states, now stepped in to put an end to the strife. Many of the hill chiefs had been elected, to the exclusion of other claimants. These disappointed rivals now came over to the Government, and brought with them a number of peons. This was the turning-point of the insurrection. The troops and their English officers, ignorant of the country and the language, could only follow the beaten tracks. These were easily obstructed by a few bamboo bushes laid across them, while here and there was a breastwork of earth and stones. Such barriers were almost impregnable without artillery, and afforded excellent shelter to the enemy. But now the aspect of affairs changed. The new recruits knew the country as well as the insurgents. They conducted the troops along scarcely practicable footpaths. Very soon their forts were reduced, the grain was captured, and the key to the position was lost to the rebels.

Events now drew rapidly to a close. In January, 1834, artillery arrived, and an attack on Jeringhi was ordered. To divert attention, an assault was made upon a small village called Ulláda, and Lieut. Sherard, of the 49th Native Infantry, was killed. On the 18th January a night attack was made on Jeringhi from three different points. Although some of the parties did not arrive till the sun was up, the attack was completely successful. The rebels fled, leaving the fort in the hands of the victors. Soon afterwards the Bissoyis of Rayagada and Lavanyakota were caught, and a month later they were hanged. Other chiefs now sued for pardon. Village after village was stormed, where the rebels still held out. They had now become desperate. They murdered or mutilated all who fell into their hands. They wounded the peasants, or cut off their noses, and sent them in to Mr. Russell, with a message that their blood was upon his head. In one village they killed or wounded twenty-six old men, women, and children.

But the end was at hand. In March, 1834, Mr. Russell obtained a notable addition in the person of one Fakir Raz. In April this man seized "Gurnall," a ferocious Savara leader, and delivered him up to justice. Then "Godeyapaud," of whom mention was made earlier, was captured, but died of a wound he received in the scuffle. The Bissani of Gumá and her sons came in and submitted; and the only rebel of consequence who was at large, was the Bissoyi of Jeringhi.

Hunted like a wild beast, he fled from one hiding-place to another. He took refuge with the Bissoyi of Tumba, and the raja, the suzerain of the latter, commanded him to deliver up the refugees. Driven thus between the devil and the deep sea—between his allegiance to his raja, and his vows of hospitality—the unfortunate Bissoyi warned his guest, and then, with the fortitude—if we may not say courage—of an ancient Roman, cut his own throat. The fugitive fled to his father-in-law, but only to bring disaster upon him, for in an attempt to seize the Bissoyi of Jeringhi, his father-in-law and his four sons were captured, while the prize escaped. The Jeringhi chief now fled northwards, and soon afterwards the Bissoyi with whom he had taken refuge, with less courage and more philosophy than his brother Bissoyi had shown, gave up his guest to the Government. One is glad to know that death spared him the disgrace of a public execution. He was placed in a false position by Major Baxter; and though he might have returned to his allegiance, he was drawn, as it were insensibly, into a rebellion to which he was originally averse.

All was over. The spirit of the revolt was broken. It remained only to dispose of the actors, as at the close of a Shakespearian tragedy, with a dead march. Eleven men were hanged, others were transported. A hundred and three of the town peons were confined. The fire was effectually put out, never to be re-lighted in Parlakimedi.

As compared with the military histories of small expeditions, the story is perhaps wanting in interest. Here and there, there was a scene which gave promise of dramatic effect; but, with the exception of the attack on Jeringhi, the war was made up of unimportant skirmishes, attacks on insignificant villages, and captures of isolated rebels. The main interest lies elsewhere. The veil is lifted, and we get a glance at district administration at that time. These things were before the days of railways or telegraphs. The post was painfully carried to Madras by runners, whose jingling rings, now a mere symbol of office, may from time to time have scared away the beasts of the jungle. Events which took place in Ganjam had passed into history before they reached the ears of Government. There was no time to obtain orders; it was necessary to act at once or never. The responsibility was increased tenfold, not only in respect of particular acts, but with regard also to the general line of action. The policy of the Government was a policy of conciliation. It was natural that the Collector should hesitate to use armed force, even at the most serious crises, and thus to commit the Government to a policy which they rejected time after time. The European officers were completely isolated. In all the events which took place before Mr. Russell's arrival we hear of only a few names—four or five at most. These few were called upon over and over again to put their lives in jeopardy, and it is to their honour, and to the credit of the service to which they belonged, that they obeyed the summons fearlessly.

But while we acknowledge the bravery of these officers, it is worthy of our remark that in no case was harm deliberately done to a European. It is true that Lieutenant Sherard was killed by a musket ball in his body, and that the wound in his arm proved fatal to Major Baxter. But the shot which killed Lieutenant Sherard was apparently fired at random in the course of a skirmish, and Major Baxter's case is hardly in point, since the advance of the troops was taken as an overt act of hostility, and the rebels probably justified his death to themselves. On the other hand, a European officer was for some time a prisoner in their hands; on more than one occasion the Collector was practically in their power, and several times English officers were surrounded by angry, threatening mobs, whose fury might have excused, though not absolved, their violence. Yet, in the midst of faction and intrigue, in the midst of burning, plundering, and mutilation, not one of these officers received any injury.

The difficulties of the enterprise are not to be measured by statistics. Judged by the number of troops engaged, by the number of men killed, or by the number of definite actions, the affair was a trifling one; but these were the very reasons why it was made so difficult. There were very few troops, and it became necessary to employ the untrustworthy town peons. If the commanders could have engaged the Bissoyi with their forces in the open plain, the disciplined troops would doubtless have soon scattered the rebels. A single battle would have decided the campaign, and, even if more blood had been spilt, the peace of the zemindari would still have been cheaply purchased. But the chieftains were too wily for that. Their dense jungles afforded them excellent cover, and they would hardly be likely to forego their advantage easily. Mr. Russell, on the other hand, was completely in the dark. We are accustomed to think of the Collectors in those days as the kings or the fathers of the people, making royal progress to receive the homage of their subjects, and listening with ready ear to the complaints of their children. The authorities in Ganjam knew nothing about the people, the country, or the language. There were no maps; there were hardly any roads. The people were either disaffected, or treacherous, or afraid. Those who should have seen that the hill tribes were a peculiar people, were treating them as the ordinary peasants of the plains. Those whose business it was to know the language of the district, did not know a word of Uriya. Those whose duties should have taken them on tours to all parts of the country, could give no information about its geography. In a word, the Intelligence Department was wanting. It did not merely fail; it never existed. The Government made a few arrests, and had perhaps produced an impression; but until the hill people were persuaded to abandon the cause of rebellion, and to become guides for the troops, the Bissoyis held their own, and success was as far off as ever.

The expedition was in many ways remarkable. Though the troops were engaged, the chief command was given to a civilian, and even when there was open war the military operations were curiously mixed with diplomacy. Now the peons were used instead of the soldiers, in the hopes of causing less irritation. Again, warfare ceased altogether, in order that the fire, unfed, might burn itself out. Anarchy had broken out fitfully for thirty-six years, and the last and most formidable insurrection lasted from September, 1831, to May, 1834! Unprovided with troops, with maps, with artillery, with information, Mr. Russell yet acted like a man who, conscious of his weakness and his difficulties, is determined to succeed in spite of both.

Most interesting of all are the Bissoyis and their hill tribes, who now for the first time came in contact with Europeans. They were a strange mixture of ferocity and shrewdness. They were ruthless in murdering men and outraging women, in plundering crops and burning villages—not because they took a delight in murder and outrage (though perhaps plunder had its own attractions), but because these things were a means to an end, and in their savage philosophy the end justified any means. On the other hand, they carried their notions of hospitality to an extreme; they were not ignorant of the arts of reading and writing, and they showed considerable skill both in their military and their diplomatic encounters with the Government. The Bissani of Gumá is described as a woman of extraordinary fascination, with the power of making every one believe her sincere—a difficult task at a time when all were treacherous. Throughout the period when the so-called "Sirdar" and his confederate were in secret league with the Bissoyis, these latter were quick to grasp the situation, and without their intelligent assistance many a well-laid plot for burning or plundering must have failed.

All this is over to-day. The jungles, which alike hid the insurgents and baffled the troops, have been cleared perhaps too effectually. Roads now run where the troops painfully followed up the scarcely distinguishable tracks. The passes are free; the forts are undefended. The officer of Government is no longer "a golden sparrow that has flown into a cage;" and, treated as a guest in the fort, he finds little in his host to remind him of the bygone ferocity of the Bissoyis of Parlakimedi.

THE LEGEND OF THE KAVERI

WHAT the Ganges is to the races of the north, that is the Kaveri to the Tamils of Southern India. Highly venerated as is the northern river, widely renowned as is the city of Benares, it may well be doubted if the river Kaveri has not obtained amongst its own devotees a veneration as high, and the shrine of Srirangam a renown as wide. To bathe in the river is forgiveness of sins; even to meditate upon it is to obtain salvation. Pilgrimages are undertaken for reasons without number: this man wishes to be cured of a terrible disease; that woman desires to be blessed in child birth; one presents his offering that his business may be successful, and another performs a sacrifice because his affairs have prospered. Extreme unction is afforded by the river, and with its water the lips of the dying are moistened.

Of all natural phenomena the Hindu loves the rivers best. Nor is this a matter for surprise. To him the river is life; from it he obtains water for drinking and for the ordinary necessities of life; by it is nourished the rice crop, which gives him the bulk of his food. Each district venerates its own river; in Tinnavelly the Tambraparni is accounted divine; in Madura the Vaigi is worshipped; but pre-eminent among them is the Kaveri, in whose adoration all the races of the south unite. It is natural that the Hindus should have endued their rivers with divine attributes, and given them a place in their theocracy, and it would be strange indeed if legends concerning them had not grown up among so imaginative a people. Thus the Vaigi of Madura was dug under the orders of a king to whom the god Krishna appeared in the form of a beggar seeking for work. And as Jason carried the goddess Hera across the foaming torrent, so the king had compassion on the beggar and set him to work in the canal. In neither case was the reward delayed. The goddess assured the hero of her protection; the grateful god dug the river Vaigi in a single day, and conferred the boon of water on the rice fields of the kingdom.

The river Kaveri rises in the mountains of Coorg, on the west coast, and, taking a general south-westerly direction, it falls into the sea in the district of Tanjore, on the east coast, after a course of about four hundred miles. Compared with the gigantic rivers of Northern

India—with the Ganges, the Indus, or the Sutlej—such a stream may appear insignificant indeed. But in point of length and breadth the Kaveri might easily hold its own among the rivers of Europe, seeing that her course is twice as long as that of the Thames, and only slightly inferior to that of the Seine. Like most Indian rivers, however, the Kaveri has the disadvantage of being wholly dry for over six months in the year. But the mission of the Kaveri is to foster agriculture and not to facilitate commerce. The river is impracticable for ships, and the whole of that sacred water is devoted to the irrigation of the land.

Leaping down from her strongholds in the mountains of Coorg, the Kaveri flows through the state of Mysore, half encircling the historic city of Seringapatam, until she emerges into the Madras Presidency in the district of Coimbatore. Gliding onwards through that district into Trichinopoly, she opens her arms to embrace the sacred fane of Srirangam, and finally pours all her accumulated wealth upon the rich alluvial plains of Tanjore, to drop at last, a tiny streamlet, into the Bay of Bengal.

It is not without reason that the Hindus revere their river, and that their imagination has woven legends about her. Even from the point of view of unromantic statistics the Kaveri is unrivalled in the south, and yields the most splendid return on the outlay in all India. In 1897–98 the area irrigated by this river in British territory was upwards of 950,000 acres. In the northern and eastern parts of Tanjore the entire land is formed by the alluvial deposit of the river. Hardly a square inch of arable land is left uncultivated, and the whole is watered by this splendid river or her tributaries.

But while the Kaveri is the source of wealth to the ryots, and of revenue to the Government, she is also the harbinger of death to the people at stated seasons of the year. No sooner has the river risen with the first floods than cholera makes its appearance. Throughout the cold season it rages, carrying off its victims by hundreds from the towns and by tens from the villages, and subsiding only with the subsidence of the river. Medical skill can only mitigate, but cannot prevent the disease. The theory that the germ is brought down by the river may not have attained the position of a well-established scientific truth, but the experiments which show that the germs are water-borne, and the coincidence of the period of the outbreak with the rise and fall of the river, go far towards proving it. By no means, however, can the natives be persuaded to give up using the water. The ignorant do not believe in what they cannot see, and argue that that water can do them no harm which they and their fathers have for ages used with impunity. The devout, if they have a lingering fear, put their soul's salvation above the risk of death, and thus the mother of the Brahmins is too often, like Saturn, the devourer of her own children.

And this is the Hindu legend of the Kaveri: There lived in the remote ages a king called Kavéra, who, by his continued austerities, had not only subdued his sensual appetites, but had even cut himself loose from all social ties. He was learned in all the learning of the Vidyas, and had attained to so sublime an ideal that human virtue itself was accounted nothing in his eyes. For a thousand celestial years he performed penance in the peaks of the Himalayas, and meditated upon the Divine essence of Bramha. At the end of that time the god, pleased with his patient devotion, appeared to him, and promised to grant him anything he might desire. "Oh, my lord," answered Kavéra, "if indeed my long penance has found favour in thine eyes, what can I desire more than release from the sorrows and the joys of this life? Let me not ask for a less abiding boon." But Bramha replied, "We Devas are not able to grant this boon. It is in the hand of one only, even the Para Bramha. But I will tell thee what I will do. My daughter, even the peerless Vishnu Maya, mother of the world, shall become thy daughter, and she shall give thee thy heart's desire." Then the god ascended into heaven and summoned Vishnu Maya, who intoxicates the world. And when the long-eyed goddess appeared, Bramha exclaimed, "Oh! happy girl, thou shalt be the daughter of this Yogi; thou shalt become a river and be called Kavéri, whereby thou shalt purify the world and lead men to heavenly bliss. Thy Divine being shall be divided in twain; as Lopamudra, thou shalt be wedded to Agastya; as Kavéri, thou shalt rule the world." With these words the god vanished.

In course of time a daughter was born to Kavéra, and grew up in the house to be the delight of her parents. The old king's asceticism now amounted to frenzy, and he announced to Kavéri his intention of forsaking the world altogether, lest any action of his should stand in the way of his salvation. Kavéri answered: "It is sufficient that I am thy daughter; I shall always proclaim thy glory, and our fathers will then attain the Para Bramha, and my sons the divine Vishnu." Kavéra then left his home, renounced all worldly affairs, and held communion with God. "He became as pure as wind, viewed the joys and sorrows of life with indifference, and thus, at the climax of his frenzy, he attained the Supreme Being."

Kavéri meanwhile was practising the austerities of her father. Vishnu appeared to her one day and said: "Kavéri, thy penance has found favour in my eyes. Ask, therefore, what boon thou wilt." Kavéri answered: "Oh, my lord! I desire to become a river, that those defiled by sin may wash in my waters and be cleansed." Then Vishnu replied, and his countenance grew black as night: "Verily it is the lot of wicked men that they should die in their sin. But thou hast asked this boon and I grant it to thee, worthless though the men be for whom thou hast asked it. Now, therefore, hearken, and I will tell thee what shall befall. In the mount of Sahya I take upon me the form of a tree, and the god Bramha will wash my feet there. In that mountain shall thy stream rise, and thou shalt flow with the waters of Bramha. Thou shalt be called the Ganges of the South, and shalt purify both gods and men. I will grant thee that thou be greater than the Ganges and chiefest among rivers, for the Ganges indeed flows from my feet, but I lie in thy lap. Moreover, Agastya will come hither bearing a pot of water. Him thou shalt wed, taking upon thee human form as Lopamudra." Then Kavéri did obeisance, and the god vanished from her eyes.

Far away to the south of the Vindhya mountains dwelt Agastya, seeking to attain salvation after the manner of holy men. But the god appeared to him and charged him to take a wife. "Be in the world," he said, "but do not loose thy hold on divine things; for better is he that feedeth a traveller at noonday, if he do not glorify himself, than he that washeth himself in the Ganges and doeth penance." But the idea of marriage was hateful to Agostya; "Why," he cried, "should I fall again into the hell of family cares?" "Verily," replied the god, "it is right to desert a wife, if she be a wretched fool or a scold. But thou shalt marry my daughter, who dwelleth in the Sahya mount." Then Agastya no longer murmured, but set out on his journey. On his way he met the Vindhya mountain, which bowed down before him, and Agastya commanded that it should not arise till he returned. But he came by another way, and thus the mountain is bowed down unto this day.

Then Agastya journeyed to the Himalayas, where he found Kavéri; and she rose up and brought water for him to drink, and bathed his feet, and did obeisance. Then Agastya said to Kavéri, "the ever-smiling, the obedient, the blue-eyed, the red-lipped, the curly-haired"—"Oh, Kavéri, I obey the god Bramha, and I have come to you. Let us therefore do as he commands." And Kavéri answered: "I am the daughter of Bramha. I am called Lopamudra, and as Kavéri I shall flow through the south. May the water of all the fourteen thousand rivers be mingled in my stream. Let the wanderer who bathes in my waters be as though he had bathed in all rivers and had performed all sacrifices. Let the land round my banks laugh; let me bring riches to the people and learning to the Brahmins. May those who perform ceremonies with my waters obtain eternal bliss. May the sins of those be forgiven who think upon my name and who look upon my stream. If thou wilt cause these things to come to pass, I will be thy wife." Then Agastya said: "This the god Bramha has promised. In this pot I carry the waters of Ganges and of the fourteen thousand rivers. A part of thee, even Kavéri, shall enter this pot, and thou, Lopamudra, shalt be my wife; and we shall journey together to the Sahya mountain. There dwells a Yogi who is Vishnu. Thou shalt be purified by the dust of his feet, and so thou shalt be the greatest of rivers, and shalt purify sinners."

Then Kavéri divided her nature and entered the pot; but as the fair maiden, Lopamudra, she stood before Agastya and did obeisance.

So the wedding was celebrated with all the magnificence that marked the nuptials of Siva and Parvati, and Bramha was present, with all the gods and the angels. Agastya bathed the feet of Vishnu and Lakshmi; the angels drank of the water, and with it the pot of Agastya was filled. And Kavéri bowed down before Parvati. Then the goddess said:—

"Always bear thyself humbly before thy husband, though he should be angry. Abstain from the society of sinners. Tell the truth, and speak mildly. Listen with joy to the renown of Vishnu. Think ever of thy husband's weal, and keep thy house as becometh a wife." So the gods and angels departed from them, and they went to the mount of Bramha. Then said

Agastya: "This is the mount of Bramha. Here will I leave the pot for a space, until I have bathed in the waters of the Swarnamukhi." Then he commanded his disciples that they should carefully guard the pot, and went to bathe in the golden-faced river.

Days went by, and he did not return. Meanwhile Kavéri remained imprisoned in the pot, but at last she said to herself: "So many days are now past, and still the Rishi does not release me. Yet he has promised to let me go, and so if I leave the pot now I shall be committing no sin."

While she was thus meditating, the god Bramha came to the mount and bathed in the golden water. Then he was aware of a tree hard by, and fell to thinking what it might be. At last he perceived that it was the god Vishnu, and he bowed down and did obeisance. Then a voice from heaven was heard: "The god Vishnu has appeared in the form of a tree. Let due worship be performed." Bramha, therefore, worshipped him with flowers and holy leaves, and bathed his feet with water from the pot. Then again the voice said: "Oh, Kavéri, thy day of happiness has come; this is the holy season in which thou shalt run to meet the sea; from henceforth thou shalt be known as the Ganges of the South. Thou shalt issue from the pot of Bramha and flow over the feet of Vishnu, and they who bathe in thy waters shall attain salvation."

And a soft wind arose, laden with sweet scents, and blew towards the south. And Indra gathered the clouds around the mountain, and a gentle rain bedewed the earth. Then did Kavéri come out of the pot; and the rain descended, and the wind blew, and she flowed forth in mighty flood to the south.

Meanwhile Agastya came in haste and found the pot fallen down. And he said to his disciples: "Whither has Kavéri fled, and why have you disobeyed your trust?" And the disciples answered, trembling: "When the storm arose, we went for shelter under the trees. Then it was that Kavéri left the pot. On her way we met her, and entreated her to return. But she heeded not, and answered: 'It is the will of the Rishi, and by the command of God I am now leaving the pot. It is in this mount I must take my source. The Rishi, who knows all things, will understand and will forgive you.' And having said this she went on her way." But Agastya, though he could not blame his disciples, was angry that the pot was lost. And Kavéri cried out: "Oh, Rishi, I knew thy will, and therefore came I out." Then

Agastya answered: "I saw thee not and I was angry. Now go thou forth and purify all the world."

So Kavéri, mingling her waters with Swarnamukhi and Kapila, flowed towards the sea. And he who feeds even one man where Kavéri joins with Kapila shall be as though he bathed in all the rivers of the world. Even a fool who bathes in these waters shall attain the Para Bramha.

And Kavéri flowed on till she reached Swethavana, and there she was wedded to Samudram (the sea). And the god Bramha appeared and gave his daughter in marriage. Flowers fell from the skies, and the angels danced in heaven; for as darkness flies at the approach of dawn, so at the thought of Kavéri does sin fly away.

Such is the legend of the Kavéri as it appears in the Sanskrit original. It seemed better not to interrupt the course of the story by stopping to elaborate the various interesting points which arise. Asceticism, which formed the last stages of the orthodox Brahmin's life, naturally plays a great part in a legend of this kind. The path to the Para Bramha leads, according to the esoteric doctrine of Brahminism, through self-restraint and mortification to the entire renunciation of the world and all its cares, its joys, and its sorrows. As it was the duty of every Brahmin to live for a period the domestic life, so also it was his duty to cast himself gradually loose from this life, and thus by the exercise of virtue and the incessant contemplation of the Divine, to reach the Para Bramha, who is perfection. Speech was denied to him, except in so far as it was necessary in reciting the Vedas. His clothing was to be the bark and the leaves of trees, and for food he was in the end to be content with what had become detached from the branches. Thus it is that the old King Kavéra is described as being "as pure as wind." The image is fine. No simile could be better than that which likens the mystical and negative state of existence which has wholly renounced all earthly intercourse, to the colourless, invisible wind, that, blowing straight from heaven, comes we know not whence, and goes we know not whither. The power acquired by the practice of austerities was immense. In the Ramayana the Kshatriya Viswamitra not only obtains the rank of Brahminhood, but even creates whole systems of stars and "afflicts the three worlds with fear." And this kind came not out but by prayer and fasting. It was Christ's doctrine of renunciation strained to the uttermost; the ideal was the annihilation of all natural feelings; they sought first, after their light, the kingdom of God and His righteousness, and trusted, not that all these things should be added unto them, but rather that that kingdom would be sufficient in itself.

The legend has probably an Aryan origin. The scenes of Kavéra's penance, of the childhood of Kavéri, and of her marriage with Agastya, is laid in the Himalayas, and in Hindustan proper. Agastya himself comes from the Deccan, and it is through him that the Kaveri is transferred to the southern country. It might be, however, that the people of the south were anxious to claim that their river also had its abode in the mountains of the gods, whence flowed the great streams of the north, and especially the Ganges. But there is a little touch in the narrative which seems to controvert this view. We are told that Kavéri was "blue-eyed, curly-haired, and red-lipped." These epithets are eminently characteristic of a northern, Aryan race, for the Dravidians themselves are generally darker in hue; amongst them blue eyes could hardly be an attribute of beauty, and red lips and curly hair are practically unknown.

The importance given to Vishnu in this legend is rather remarkable. The worship of Vishnu predominates in the north, and especially in Orissa, where the great temple of Jagannath stands, and where Siva is adored in the shape of a single stone in temples placed outside the villages. In the south the people are generally worshippers of Siva; and though there are many temples to Vishnu, the greatest are dedicated to Siva, or his son, or his wife. All the people of the south alike reverence the Kaveri. The temple at Madura, however, belongs to Mariamman, that at Trichendur in Tinnevelly holds Subramaniam in honour. At the holy, "Thula," week, when the people flock to Mayavaram to obtain the special purification of the Kavéri, Subramaniam, Siva's son, is worshipped under the form of Mayuram. But although Vishnu appears in this legend as superior to Bramha, who washes his feet, we find that at the wedding it is Parvati, the wife of Siva, to whom Kavéri does obeisance, and who gives her the parting words of advice. It is therefore probable that we should not consider the legend wholly Vaishnava or wholly Saiva. It perhaps belongs equally to both creeds, though Vishnu plays the more important part. There are, moreover, temples in the south where both deities are worshipped alike. And it is to be noticed also that the god Bramha appears more than once. It is he that promises to give the divine Maya as a daughter to Kavéra, and he also appears at her wedding with the sea. This is the more remarkable because at the Sahya mount he is described, as I have said, as washing the feet of Vishnu, and this would seem to imply inferiority. Bramha must not, however, be confounded with the Para Bramha of the Upanishads, the incarnation of all perfection and the ideal of esoteric Brahminism. Indeed the distinction is drawn by Bramha himself, where he says that death is a boon which is not for the Devas to give, being in the hands of the Para Bramha alone.

The domestic aspect of the legend is also not without its interest. Homely touches and somewhat ludicrous incidents are not uncommon in ancient writings. Hera is suspended from heaven in a golden chair, and Ares roars with pain, "like ten thousand bulls!" The gods of the Chaldean mythology swarm to the sacrifice "like flies," and crouch like frightened dogs before the gate of Anu. In this legend we find Bramha propounding a new theory of divorce. "It is right," he says, "to desert a wife, if she be a wretched fool or a scold." And Parvati enumerates to Kavéri her housewifely duties. "It is your husband's right to be angry," she says in effect, "and it is for the wife to bear it in silence. The husband must always be first in his wife's thoughts; and next to domestic duties comes the love of truth and religion." This insistence on the subordination of woman, even though she be divine, is to be expected in Hindu writings. Sita's fame in the Ramayana is not more due to her chastity when in Ravana's power than to her wifely devotion to Rama in the forest.

But the most striking conception in the legend is the dual nature ascribed to Kavéri. There is no materialism in this. Kavéri and Lopamudra are not two separate embodiments of a common original; they are essentially the same person. The writer has evidently some difficulty in maintaining the metaphysical idea, for, though Kavéri enters the pot, and Lopamudra journeys with her husband, yet, when Kavéri starts on her course to the east, Agastya, it seems, is left alone. Yet when Kavéri reaches the sea she is wedded to him, and this would imply that she has an existence altogether distinct from Lopamudra, the wife of Agastya. One is reminded of the Christian Faith, which declares that, "although He be God and man, yet He is not two, but one Christ." This doctrine is also not unknown to the metaphysics of the Indian sages. In the Brihadaranyaka

Upanishad Self is declared to have existed in the beginning in the form of the Purusha or Person. "He was as large as man and wife together. He then made his self to fall into two, and thence arose husband and wife. He embraced her, and men were born. She thought, 'How can he embrace me after having produced me from himself? I shall hide myself.' She then became a cow, the other became a bull, and embraced her, and hence cows were born." In like manner she became the female and he the male, until the creation of all things that have sex was complete. The Purusha is not made up of two component parts, the man and the woman. His personality remains the same after the creation of woman and the animals as before it, just as Kavéri and Lopamudra, while they have separate existence, are manifestations of the same person. The same idea seems to be more clearly expressed in the account of creation in the Aitareya Upanishad, where the Purusha is described as the First Cause in human form, from whose members proceed the elements, the heavenly bodies, and the trees. These deities re-enter the sentient being, man, in various forms, Agni, the fire, becoming speech; Vayu, the air, the breath of the nostrils; Aditya, the sun, his eyes, and so forth.

Though the main features of the legend are preserved, the common people have many variations of the details. According to one version, when Agastya left the pot on the ground near the tree of Vishnu, a crow came and perched on it: the pot fell over, and the water of the Kaveri began to flow. This variation is not authentic, and is in every way inferior to the Sanskrit story. The birth of the Kaveri is here attributed to a vulgar accident, while in the authentic version, the natural picture of the burst of the rains is adorned with poetical image—the coyness of Kavéri and the gentle presence of Indra and the wind god, growing more boisterous as the storm increases.

In the district of Tanjore, and not many miles from the mouth of the Kaveri, the river is remarkable for its winding course, and in one place it actually runs to the west. The people of those parts say that here Agastya came near to catching the truant, and that she was forced to wind about in her efforts to escape. It is plain, however, that this is a variation, for, according to the original legend, we find Agastya on the Sahya mount, at first angry, but afterwards bowing to the will of God, nor does he make the least attempt to follow Kavéri. The variation, moreover, has probably arisen in the locality, and was especially suggested by the doubling back of the river upon itself. The wedding of Kavéri and the sea took place, not at Kaveripatnam (Kavéri's town), which lies at the present mouth of the river, but at a place nearly nine miles inland. This fact points to the antiquity of the legend, and also to the rapid formation of the delta. The forces of nature have, however, been materially helped by the extension of irrigation farther up the river. No doubt the Kaveri, originally, had a considerable estuary, and this probably gave to Kaveripatnam its reputation as an ancient and flourishing port. Now, however, when almost all the water is drained away for purposes of agriculture, the river dwindles in the course of fifty miles from a considerable stream to a tiny rivulet not more than twenty yards across, and the contraction has, of course, led to the formation of land.

The mention of Kaveripatnam suggests that this is a fitting place to tell the story connected with that village, though it is entirely separate from the legend of the river. Kaveripatnam, now a poor little fishing village, and insignificant even among villages, was once the abode of royalty, and traded in gold and precious stones. The court was splendid ; the buildings were magnificent, and a stately fleet of merchantmen rode at anchor in the mouth of the river. The prosperity has long since passed away; the oracles, with more logic and less ambiguity than is generally to be found in them, declared that on the day when the great irrigation dams were begun their city would be destroyed. Even now, however, great blocks either of brick or stone remain to witness to the glory that has departed, and the natives say that at times an uncut ruby may be picked up among the *débris*. The place is desolate; the monotony of the sand heaps, so common along the Coromandel coast, is broken by trees, which look forlorn when contrasted with the general luxuriance of the delta. Even the prickly pear, at all times dusky and uncompromising, seems to have taken on a dingier hue and a more uncompromising character. On the dreary sea-shore a few huts huddled together and a few nets spread out to dry attest the existence of a petty trade, sole remnants of the commerce of a once flourishing town.

Long ago, before the city had risen into grandeur, there lived an aged fisherman and his wife. And one day a stranger arrived at their hut, bearing with him a bundle, which he laid upon the threshold. He told the dame to guard the bundle well, for in it she would find her fortune, and having said this he vanished.

The old woman unrolled the bundle, and in it she found a baby boy. She took him up and nursed him, and he grew up with them. Time went on, and the affairs of the old couple had prospered, until they found themselves the owners of several large boats. Meanwhile the child had grown into a handsome boy of fourteen, and his foster father, judging that the mysterious child had brought with him the blessing of prosperity, had suspicions that he was more than mortal. So convinced was he of this, that he put the boy in command of the boats, and told the sailors to do whatever he should order. Accordingly the boats put out to sea, and all went well until they touched at a port. Then the boy captain told them to fill the vessels with mud, but the sailors, surprised at such an absurd order, at first refused to comply. Some of the wiser among them, however, remembering the injunction laid upon them by the master, persuaded their comrades to obey, and soon the crews were engaged in the ridiculous task of loading their boats with mud. Many were the misgivings as the boats sailed for home, and loud were the murmurs that the master was nothing better than a fool, in having sent a mere lad in command of his vessels. But when they reached home, lo! all the mud was changed into solid gold. The boy was revealed to his astonished foster parents as the god Subramaniam, the Divine son of Siva and Parvati. Then he was caught up into heaven, leaving behind him a promise of his favour to the aged couple and of assured prosperity to the town of Kaveripatnam.

FISHERMEN ON THE EAST COAST

At Kynance Cove, not two miles from the Lizard, they show you a rock, in which are a few tiny basins of water known as the fish pools. They are simply hollows in the rock, the largest some two feet square and as many deep, but in them dwells a community of small fish, unconscious of the waste of waters outside, of wrecks, of storms, and of the continual warfare between man and their larger brethren of the ocean. There they live their tranquil lives, surrounded on all sides by protecting walls, and above them only the clear water and the sky. The tide comes in and recedes again, and if from time to time an individual be missing, the community remains undisturbed by tides and unharmed by man, for the people of the coast will not touch them. At times a commotion arises, when some unhappy mollusc is dropped into the pool to make sport for a wanton boy or a curious visitor. In such a case the water is alive with flashing tails. The more fortunate fasten on the unlucky shellfish; others dart about, looking in vain for a place where they too can take hold. For a few moments the whole community is in a ferment; then the excitement is over, and once more the pool is at rest.

Such is the life of the fisher folk of Tranquebar. For scores of years they have lived their placid life in the village, undisturbed by the coming of the white man—hardly conscious of the change of masters, or of the fortunes which have overtaken their native place. For Tranquebar was once the "Queen of the East." She owed her being to the colony which was sent out from Denmark by King Frederick IV., and whose church bears the royal monogram to this day. In the times of Christiern VII. a fort arose on the sea beach. The high road led through a stately gate, down the royal street (still named after the king) to Government House, which was separated from the fort by the Grand Square. Ships then came to Tranquebar, bringing, not perhaps "ivory, apes, and peacocks," but the articles of a more practical commerce. Loves, hates, and intrigues worked themselves out in the Palace, in the Square, in the Fort. And then, in 1845, the Danes and their following disappeared, like Galuppi's audiences, "with lives that came to nothing, or with deeds as well undone." Only the plant of their religion they left to the care of the Leipzig Mission. For in 1845 Tranquebar was sold by treaty to the British, and a new generation arose under new auspices. Hither came the revenue officers and other high officials of the Government, bringing with them those whose business brought them into frequent contact with the various parts of the administration. The fort was turned into a jail; Government House became a court of justice, over which the District Judge presided. But these, too, passed away. Trade now flows to a neighbouring and more convenient port. Government House has dwindled to a petty post-office; the fort is degraded to a mere custom-house, and out on the Square the remnant of the surrounding pillars are as the tombstones of the gallants and ladies who once walked there in the cool of the evening.

But the fisher folk live on their tranquil life, unconscious of these changes. Their ideas are limited to the narrow circle in which they live; their interests are centred wholly in the catching of fish, or in the making and mending of boats and nets. From time to time a commotion arises among them. Some adventurous member has gone on that mysterious voyage to the "Islands"—the Atlantis of the East Coast peasant; and when he returns the community fastens upon him, devouring eagerly every scrap of the news he brings. For nine days the wonder lasts; then the excitement subsides, and the life sinks back once more into its placid routine.

In accordance with the Hindu economy, the fishermen form a caste by themselves, and they are very low in the social scale. Those who live in the extreme south are indeed Christians, whose forefathers were converted to the faith by St. Francis Xavier. They are devout Catholics, and they have preserved the Portuguese names by which their fathers were baptized into the Church, so that, incongruous as it sounds, José Fernandez and Maria Santiago are but humble folk, catching fish in a primitive way, with no more clothing on than a small loin cloth and a picture of the Virgin. Farther up the coast, and in Tranquebar, of which we are speaking, the fisher folk are Hindus, and caste has the effect, which, however lowly it be, it always has, of uniting the community in the bonds of brotherhood. They choose out from among them a man of influence, or of wealth, to lead them, and then they band together in little groups of four or five for fishing purposes, though the whole community is one and indivisible, and though each man has his separate place in it. Each man, too, has his own fishing net, and probably his own small canoe, and may, if he prefers it, go out alone. Most men, however, prefer to join one or other of the groups, for company's sake, and also for profit. The laws of the little republic are well understood, though unwritten; and they work without friction. The younger men do the hard work—reef the sails, row from one fishing ground to another, let down and haul up the great seines; it is the part of the elder men to guide the boats, to choose the best ground, and to control the working of the nets. Before the rim of the sun appears on the horizon above the edge of the water, they are astir, running out the canoes, collecting the nets, and preparing the tackle. All the morning they fish, and the more industrious remain until the sun sinks behind the fringe of cocoanut trees that marks the coast-line of their village. But in stormy weather, when the rain is beating down on the water, and the waves are tossing their light canoes like cockle-shells, they do not venture out at all, or they do not stay out so long, for the fish then seek the deeper water, the risk to man and boats and tackle is greater, and the profit is less considerable. And when they are back ashore, the fish are handed over to the women, and the solitary amusement of the evening begins. For the fishermen drink a great deal. They justify the indulgence to themselves, by saying that their hard life in the salt waters makes stimulants a necessity; and perhaps they are not altogether wrong. In fact, half their earnings goes in this way, and they would spend more if they could afford it. "What do you do if you earn a rupee?" a man was asked. "How do you spend it?" "Eight annas goes to buy rice," he replied, "and eight annas to buy toddy." "And what if you earn another rupee?" "Buy more drink," was the ingenuous answer. But though they are so fond of intoxicants, it would be unfair to describe them as a class given to drunkenness. Cocoanut toddy is a comparatively mild form of stimulant, and long habit and hard work has probably weakened the effect of the alcohol.

It is the part of the men to catch the fish and to bring them home; the women's business is to take the fish to market and sell them. Once the haul is ashore and the women have taken charge of it, the men put aside all thoughts of fish and fishing till the next morning. So little do they know of the market values that they could not tell off-hand the price of a particular fish or of a particular haul. They are content to hand over the catch to their wives and to receive whatever they may get for it. They do not generally keep much for their own consumption, for they prefer rice; perhaps they have a natural disgust for what they are so closely and so constantly connected with.

The morning I had fixed on for my excursion dawned bright and clear. Though the sun was rising behind a bank of clouds the sky gave promise of a glorious day, and a cool, fresh breeze blew invitingly off the sea. Down in a backwater lay our boat, just out of reach of the breaking waves. They had made ready for me a luxurious ship, by the simple contrivance of tying two large canoes together; and on this lordly vessel was placed the chair of state, for the native in Southern India seems to think an Englishman can do nothing without a chair. Whether he goes out to inspect crops, or to superintend some irrigation work; whether he is going a-fishing or a-hunting, the inevitable chair is borne before him, often to the sole discomfort of the bearer, for, of course, it is seldom used. Still, it takes the place of a standard, and perhaps adds some dignity to the cavalcade in the eyes of those whom it is meant to impress.

In the boat, however, the chair was not of much advantage, for the means of fastening it down were scanty, and the equilibrium of the boat was such as to make one prefer a safer, if less dignified position. I had taken the precaution to dress in character, for the chances of getting wet are not small when your boat has no sides, even though the seas may not be running high. And now fairly on board we began to slip down the backwater towards the breakers. For one moment the boat held her breath, as she mounted the white crest of an advancing wave. Then she plunged forward, and we were through the foam with hardly a splash, and making for the open sea.

The word "catamaran," as every one knows, is made up of two Tamil words meaning "trees bound together;" and the description is as literal as it is concise. The boats consist simply of two rough-hewn logs tied together with rope. They are slightly curved at stern and bow, to lessen in some degree the resistance of the water, but this is all that distinguishes them from an ordinary raft. On his logs the fisherman squats, and paddles his craft along after the fashion of a Canadian canoe. His oars are as rude as his boat; to a thin rough-hewn pole is tied, by means of a rope and two holes bored in it, a flat, circular piece of wood, to serve as a blade. In front of the rower are piled his nets and his line, and there, too, he deposits the fish he catches. Yet, primitive as the vessel is, nothing could serve his purposes better. The man is practically naked, and he is as much at home in the water as out of it. If a heavy sea washes him off his seat he has but to clamber back into it, for the boat cannot easily be upset, and, if it were, it is almost as serviceable bottom upwards! True, he may lose his nets, and his fish, if he have caught any; but these are easily replaced, and perhaps the greatest misfortune would be to lose his oar. It is seldom or never that a fisherman loses his life; in addition to his great powers of swimming, and to the handiness of his boat, he can always reckon on the assistance of his companions, for the sense of brotherhood is strong among these fisher folk. Not only are they bound together by the ties of a common caste and a common profession, but they have early learnt the advantage of division of labour. Each is necessary to the other, for a big net worked by several canoes will give each man a profit he could not hope to realize by his unaided efforts.

Many of the canoes are larger than the one described, and boast of sail, rudder, and oars. Except that the number of logs is increased, the hull is built in exactly the same way; on to the stern is tied a piece of wood, rudely shaped into the resemblance of a rudder. The oars are bound to the sides of the craft, but not so tightly as to interfere with their free play, and the ropes that bind them thus serve the purposes of rowlocks. There is perhaps nothing remarkable in this, for even on such civilized waters as the Norway fiords the fishermen are accustomed to use loops of rope, in which they insert the oars, and, clumsy though they seem to the inexperienced—*mihi crede experto*—practice has made them effective enough to the Norwegian boatmen. The sail and mast, which match the rest of the vessel in rudeness of construction, are hoisted into a socket, where the mast is kept in its place by the assistance of two or three of the crew. Arrived at the fishing ground, the boat is made fast by a primitive anchor, consisting of a heavy stone tied to the end of a long rope. The whole vessel might be taken for the model of a prehistoric yacht, the first link in the long chain of evolution, of which the last is the modern racing cutter. All is sufficiently complete; the principles of the sailing vessel are all recognized. Means are provided for steering, for anchoring, for tacking; the bow is raised to present less surface to the water; oars are ready to provide for the absence of wind. But on board such a vessel you feel as though transported into another epoch—past the long Dragon ships of the Vikings, past the battleships of the Peloponnesian war, past even the "black ships" of the Homeric ages. On such a boat as ours was, the desperate victims of Noah's flood might have made a vain effort to save themselves. Yet even they would have devised some method of fixing the mast in its place; for of all that is primitive about the boat, surely the most primitive contrivance is the use of human support for the mast! However, the men employed in this way would have nothing else to do while the boat is under sail, so that the inconvenience is probably not considerable.

Meanwhile we were sliding out to sea, and the rowers had taken their oars and were putting their backs into it. The crew consisted of four or five rowers, the master (who took the helm), and a boy-of-all-work, an apprentice, perhaps, and the son of one of the sailors. All were entirely naked, save for the merest shred of cloth, which cut decency down to its narrowest limit. Before long the steersman struck up a ditty, and all the rowers joined in the chorus. It is the delight of all natives working in unison. Their bodies swing in time with the rhythm, and their spirits rise with the mere exercise of shouting. There is a tacit understanding amongst them, for, when one is evidently tiring, by reason of the great strain on the voice, another takes up the wondrous tale, as though it were his part in the play. What the song was, and what the tune was, were matters of mere conjecture, but the chorus was plain enough. "Velu Mayilu," they sang at their oars; "oh Subramaniam, Lord of the Peacock, hear us." So we may suppose that the poem was originally a "hymn to Siva's son," but has degenerated into a mere time-keeper for the oars and an encouraging noise for the rowers. Not otherwise does the piano-organ or the German band degrade the great productions of a European master into mere noisy importunities for coppers.

And when the hymn was finished, there was silence for a while, broken only by the regular plash of the oars. Then the song broke out again, this time some local ditty about the coming of the English to Tranquebar—

"The waves lapped the black ship that brought the strangers to the Indian strand."

In truth, the jargon is such that their own people cannot understand it. The words are lost in the riot of their lusty voices, as well as in the incomprehensible dialect, and only by dint of careful listening is a chance phrase picked up from time to time. And now we had left Tranquebar far behind, and the shore began to be a mere fringe of cocoanut palms, broken only in one place by the mass of the Danish fort. But the breeze was beginning to freshen, and it was time to hoist sail. Up it went, with plenty of noise, of advice it may be, and of objurgation also. We slipped merrily through the dancing water, the rude sail bellying to the wind, while the efforts of its human supports could hardly hold the mast in its place. And as we went, the small fry of the ocean, seen clearly through the transparent water, flitted round us, secure in their own insignificance. Soon there came floating by a huge shapeless mass of dead white jelly, and at once one of the young fishermen jumped into the water after it: not that the ugly mass has a market value, he was simply trying to gratify my curiosity. But when he had laid hold of it, he cried out and made at once for the boat. Flinging the thing on board, and scrambling hastily up after it, he fell to rubbing his naked body and chest vigorously with salt water. For the thing stung like a nettle, and the irritation, if superficial, is none the less painful.

And now we and our attendant canoes had reached the fishing grounds, and the big boat dropped her stone anchor. Then the net was unwound, and each canoe, taking hold of it, rowed out in different directions from the parent boat, so that at last a large circle was formed, which was covered by the net stretched out under the water. Far away the canoes lay, with nothing to mark their connection with the bigger boat, except the nodding floats that dotted the water between, and marked where the fatal net was spread. But at a signal from the leader, all rowed once more together, bringing the great net with them, until they were again collected in a little crowd. And then, with shouts and cries, some giving advice, and others yelling for yelling's sake, up rushed the big net through the swirling water, until at last the end came, and at the bottom, with the sand and slime, and shell, there was a wriggling, glistening mass of silver, and pink, and brown—sea-snakes and eels, fish great and small, crabs and prawns, all mingled together in one writhing confusion. Afterwards began the task of sorting; the sea-snakes were thrown back to liberty, as well as such of the small fish as would not serve for bait. Prawns are of little account for the market, but they are the food of many larger fishes, and are therefore much used in line fishing. Again and again the same process is repeated, and now and then a prize is taken in the shape of a pomfret or a seer. But too often the net contains nothing but small fry and shell-fish, which, though saleable in the market, are hardly worth the trouble of sorting. And when the little fleet has sufficiently swept that ground, and the profits of the net become less and less, it moves off perhaps to some other fishing ground, or each canoe will go off to fish with line and bait on its own account. Long practice has, of course, taught the fisherman where to cast his net, and where to take to his line. Chiefly, perhaps, out of courtesy to myself, our boat went off to one of the line fishing grounds, and there we fished with hooks driven through the backs of live prawns and small fish. We were not, however, very successful, for, though the fish rose at the bait in sufficient quantity, they were all insignificant in size. Line fishing is always a slower process, but there is a greater chance of a big prize.

Of the fish that are caught off the coast, the pomfret and the seer are the most profitable. All European tables know well the white and delicate flat fish, as well as the equally white and firmer flesh of the seer. Sometimes a shark comes by and takes the bait; but this is not common, and man-eating sharks especially are said to be very rare. It is considered very ill-omened to catch a shark, and the line which has been the cause of such a misfortune is thrown away. This, however, is no great hardship, and perhaps the superstition has grown out of what was at first only a convenience. For the shark, which would be an unwelcome passenger on the small canoe, has to be cut adrift, and the hook with it. So that the severed line would, in all circumstances, be of little use. It is rather strange, however, that, except this one superstition, I was only able to find one legend concerning the fish, and that had a Christian origin. It is said that St. Francis Xavier, walking one day along the shore, engaged in devotions, dropped his rosary. A wave swept it away, and it was seen no more. But while he was searching for it a crab came up to him, bearing it in his mouth. Overjoyed at the recovery of the rosary, and considering that the crab was obeying a Divine command, St. Francis blessed the creature with the sign of the cross, and this sign it wears to this day. The crab is said to be common only along the east coast near Tranquebar, and it goes by the name of the Catholic crab.

But the sun was getting hot, and we were three miles from the shore. I, too, had the work of the day before me, and, pleasant as was the cool green water, it was time to weigh anchor and hoist sail. So we ran back without adventure to the shore, where I parted from my hosts. They started again for the fishing grounds, in hopes of better luck, and I returned to my camp, not ill-pleased with my morning's experience in a catamaran.

TRADITION IN SOUTH INDIA

A HALO of romance and poetry will always linger about the East, as long as the palm trees wave and the sun continues to set. It is the land of awful and ancient religions, of magnificent ceremonial, and of immemorial custom. On the other hand, the Hindu in public life, be he administrator, magistrate, or pleader, conducts his business after the prosaic method of the West; he has nothing Oriental about him save his dress and his inviolable caste. The peasant works out his appointed time in the monotonous routine of village life; he lives in his fields, moves in his bullocks, and has his being in never-ending conversations about money, markets, lawsuits, and the price of land.

We are permitted to see but little of the domestic life—that inner sanctuary, which the Hindu guards with such zealous care. Sometimes a corner of the veil is lifted, and we may, if we choose to look, obtain a glimpse of that which lies beyond. We may see that the contract of marriage is not a mere agreement by the husband to maintain his wife, and by the wife to cook her husband's food and to bear his children. We may see the father, when he has finished his day's work and put off all but the most necessary raiment, take his child upon his knee, and untying the knot of his hair, twist it round his face, so as to represent a bogie, and to frighten the boy into a delicious ecstasy of terror. At times the boys may be seen playing their game of blind man's buff, where the protagonist, instead of having his eyes bandaged, is bound to hold his breath while he catches his companions. Every morning the girls are drawing in pounded rice wonderful freehand designs at the threshold of their homes. But these are slender signs. Too often Indifference guards the gate of Affection, and Respect puts on the likeness of Servility.

Fables, myths, legends, and superstitions—by whatever name we call them—are interesting, firstly, because they embody the immemorial wisdom of the ancients; secondly, because they afford assistance to the scholar in tracing the connection between East and West; and, thirdly, in that they shed a light, however dim, upon the everyday life of the people. The philosophy of the ages soon settled upon the infinite problem of the beginning of things, and the result was a fable, a theory, a narrative, suited to the ethical character of the nation which conceived it. The Greeks divided the rule of the upper world, the sea, and the infernal regions, among a Trinity who had forcibly supplanted an ill-defined race of giants, children of the union between the primeval Heaven and Earth, themselves the offspring of Chaos and Night. The Hebrews, with a more forcible philosophy, imagined that the world fell into order out of chaos at the bidding of an Omnipotent Spirit. The Brahmin doctrines ascribe the creation to a Primal Being, brooding over the waste of waters, from whom proceeded in due course the elements, the sun and moon, and lastly man. All Nature became transformed by the imagination of these old races. A perennial fountain becomes a mother mourning for her children, slain by the sun-god, whose rays are arrows in his hand. The woods and fountains are peopled with oreads and satyrs and naiads, and the sea is the abode of nereids and tritons. And in the robuster legends of Scandinavia, the earth is a giant, whose valleys are the scars left by the mighty strokes of Thor's hammer; the sea is a drinking cup, which he tries in vain to drain; and the valkyrs ride on the storm-clouds to the field of battle, and carry the valiant dead to Valhalla.

Amongst the Hindus, besides the religious stories, which go to make up much of the folk lore, we find also fables of the doings of animals, and of the origin of birds and trees. These myths, which for the most part wrap up some wise reflection in the palatable form of anecdote, often had their origin or their counterpart in the ancient Sanskrit writings. The dainty French milkmaid, whose unguarded toss of the head upset both her milk and her calculations, has been traced for us by Professor Max Müller through the Arab whose stick, intended for the back of a visionary son, destroyed his pot of honey, to the Sanskrit Brahmin, who, less careful of domestic reverence, kicked at an imaginary wife, and found her but a bag of rice. The philologist has used the fable as an example of the connection between Eastern and Western lore, and also of the variations which such fables undergo in the course of their journey. To us, who are rather considering the point of interest, I have placed third, the three stories of the milkmaid, the Arab, and the Brahmin are each characteristic of the people and of the age to which they belong. The milkmaid upsets her milk with a gesture truly French; but while the Arab chastises his *son* with a stick, the Brahmin corrects his *wife* with a more humiliating foot. Of the age, therefore, and not of the people alone, for we have not from this story occasion to represent the Brahmin of to-day as treating his wife otherwise than with respect.

But besides the two great classes of religious legends and of philosophic aphorisms, there is the third division, which we call fairy tales, nursery rhymes, and ghost stories. The natives of South India do not seem to have nursery rhymes, properly so called. My judgment, however, remains at present in suspension, for I do not wish to infer that what I have not been able to find is therefore non-existent. But when I asked what children had in the way of stories, I was given a long tale of a king and his ministers, in which the gods duly figured, and (to the best of my belief) a Lady of the Lake played some part. Such a tale is very far from "Little Miss Muffet," or the cow which jumped over the moon, but no effort of mine could discover anything analogous to these. No Indian maiden sat on a "tuffet," or even a mat, to drink her milk or her rice water; no Hindu Jack Horner squatted in any corner to pick out the best of the sweetmeats, and to praise himself for the act. Instead of these the children are generally fed with the ever new adventures of Rama, or with stories of beasts and birds from the Panchatantra, which are not really nursery tales, but rather belong to the second class, that is, the class of moral fables.

Some analogy, at least of horror, may perhaps be traced between the wicked wolf of Little Red Riding Hood and the were-tiger, that gruesome idea, which seems to have taken fast hold of the imagination of Oriental and of half barbarous nations. Some such idea seems to be latent in the following story: Once upon a time a tiger fell in love with a beautiful maiden, who lived in a village near the hills where his lair was. So he took upon himself the form of a handsome youth and went to ask her in marriage of her parents. The old people, not suspecting anything, and overjoyed at finding such a suitor for their daughter's hand, readily consented, and the wedding took place in due course. Two or three days after the festivities were over, husband and wife started to walk to their home. The way was long, and the woman began to flag. "Let us rest here, dear husband," she said, "for I am tired." But he answered roughly, "Be quiet, or else I shall show myself in my true shape." So she trudged along for some time in silence, but at last she complained again. When he answered her as before, she met him with defiance and, like Semele, in the Greek legend, insisted on seeing his true form. Then the human disguise fell off, and a tiger stood before her. She was struck dumb with fright, but what could she do? She was alone in the jungle, far from her house and from all human habitation, and there was nothing for it but to follow her terrible lord. At last they arrived at the lair in the heart of the jungle, and there she set about putting the house in order. Meanwhile the tiger, in pity for the poor girl, had resumed his human shape, and never again appeared before her as a tiger. So they lived together for two years, and two children were born to them, which, however, were neither more nor less than tiger cubs.

Meanwhile the woman grew restless, and said to her husband, "Dear husband, it is long since I have seen my parents and my brothers. Let me go, if only for a few days, and see how they do." But her husband, knowing that this would be the end of their union, refused to let her go. Several times she asked his leave, and as often as she asked she was refused. At last she determined to fly; so one day, when her husband had gone out to hunt, she took a knife and stabbed the cubs, and having hung the bodies from the roof directly over a hot iron plate, she locked the door and ran off through the jungle to her native village at the top of her speed, not daring so much as to look behind her.

In due course the tiger came home in the evening and knocked at the door, but, as he could get no answer and could not open the door, he listened at the keyhole and heard the hiss of the blood as it fell drip, drip, on the hot iron plate. At first he thought his wife was too busy preparing the evening cakes to attend to his knocking, but at last, as he could not make her hear, he was obliged to force open the door. And what a sight met his eyes! His two cubs hung from the roof dripping with blood, and his wife had vanished!

Next morning he went off in human shape to his father-in-law to fetch his wife back, and was met by her brothers, who courteously welcomed him to a sumptuous repast. When the meal was over, he was asked to sit down on a mat, while the brothers offered him the customary courtesy of betel leaves. Suspecting nothing, he stepped on to the mat, and tumbled into the pit over which it had been laid. Then the treacherous brothers, who had previously made ready a heap of stones, stoned him to death as he lay in the pit. And that was the end of the tiger.

Though the idea of a were-tiger seems to underlie this story, the positions are reversed; for while we are accustomed to hear of the man, who takes upon himself at will the form of a beast, we have here a tiger who can at pleasure assume the form of a man. All our sympathies, however, are with the tiger, for if he deceived the girl at first, he was, in the end, more sinned against than sinning. The brothers, moreover, cannot be acquitted of the cardinal sin of killing a guest by treachery, even though the guest was a tiger. The native theory, however, seems to be that the were-tiger and all of his race must be destroyed at all costs, and that the end justifies any means.

Far more weird is the Malay story of the real were-tiger*—the beast who destroyed cattle, and was himself caught in a trap. Step by step they tracked the blood, till it led them to the house of a man, and there their marrow froze and their hair stood erect. They could not seize him, and from that time the man disappeared, but folk say he limped to his dying day. The idea, also, of the souls of men inhabiting

* Hugh Clifford, "In Court and Kampong."

beasts, which is probably an offshoot of the were-tiger tradition, is to be found amongst the Uriyas, who will not shoot bears, lest they should contain the soul of a grandmother! The were-animal is known to most of the ruder nations, but the more refined mythology of Greece does not seem to have admitted the idea. Zeus, indeed, assumes the form of a bull when courting Europa, and the Centaurs were half beast. But Zeus was a god, whose ethereal substance could assume any form, and who was above mere human laws; and there is no reason to suppose that the Centaurs could change their shapes. The story of Circe, again, and with it "Beauty and the Beast," and the many German tales of enchanted princes must be distinguished on the ground that in these last the man assumes bestial form at the bidding of another. While he is under the spell, he is powerless to help himself, and he can regain human shape only by the favour of the wizard or by the intervention of a third person. The were-man, on the contrary, could assume the form of a wolf or tiger, or put it off, as it suited his convenience. For a true analogy we must turn to the "Volsung Saga," where Sigmund and Sinfiotli grew—

"As very wolves
In outward shape and semblance, and they howled out wolfish
things,
Like the grey dogs of the forest, though somewhat the heart of kings
Abode in their bodies of beasts."

The East probably gave birth to a tradition, which appears in less savage forms amongst many of the nations of Europe, and especially among the Scandinavian and Teutonic races. From this fable we pass on to the more common kind of moral story, which has its closest analogy in the fables of Æsop. These are, moreover, in entire accord with the Hindu genius, and the "Panchatantra" furnishes many examples. The well-known "ass in the lion's skin" reappears with characteristic variations in the following :—

An ass once put on a tiger skin, and used to graze every day in the rice field. The owner, taking him for a tiger, dared not disturb him. But one day a fox (or more probably a jackal), being maliciously inclined, said, "Uncle, it is long since I heard the sweet tones of your voice. Pray sing a little." The ass brayed, and the owner, seeing the trick, promptly killed him with sticks and stones.

Æsop, who differs from this story in details, which are easily referred to geographical causes, lacks the insensibility to the feelings of animals which the Hindu fable betrays. That this is entirely in keeping with the Hindu character, those can testify who have seen a driver belabour an overladen horse, or a coolie carry a pig, slung head downwards on a pole. Nay, the cow herself, the mother of Brahmins, or at least the bull, beloved of Siva, is not treated with the respect due to the sacred animal of the East. I do not speak, of course, of those holy kine which are free to roam the streets, or to lie lazily flicking the flies off them in hospitable verandahs, or devouring dainties, willingly offered, for that the finger of God is on them. These are the high priesthood of the cattle, but their humbler working brethren are treated with singular indifference.

Save for its likeness to, and its variations from, the story of Æsop, this fable (and indeed the one which follows) must not be regarded as especially interesting in itself, but rather as a type of many such stories of animals, which I have chosen simply because it was told me by one of the people. It has at any rate the old moral attached, but it is difficult to see what lesson, except the obvious one of using common sense, we are to learn from the fable of the monkey and the crocodile.

There was once a monkey, which lived on the banks of a great river, feeding on the luscious fruit of a tree that grew there. A crocodile observing this, and thinking that a monkey which lived so well would be a dainty mouthful, watched for an opportunity to catch him. So one day, when the monkey came to drink, the crocodile seized him and carried him off to the middle of the river. Arrived there, she said, "Aha! good sir, shall I tell you why I have brought you here? I have long thought that you would be a dainty morsel, and now I shall have a fine feast on your heart and liver." "Oh, mother," replied the monkey, "why did you not tell me this before? I would gladly have given you my heart and liver, but I am sorry to say I left them on the tree! If you take me back, I will let you have them at once." The crocodile believed this, and carried him to the shore; and the monkey, jumping off his back, was soon up a tree. "O fool," he cried to her, "to suppose I could leave my heart behind me!"

Many and varied are the legends which belong to the naming of villages or to the origin of rivers. The story of the Kaveri has been told at length, and need not be repeated. Of the Coleroon, whose name signifies "killing," they tell the following :—

A mother was wearily trudging over the burning sands with her child in her arms. Overcome by fatigue, she laid the child down and went aside to rest. But the god came down in the floods of the river and snatched the child away.

The names of villages are often derived from local legends, but unfortunately the traditions have too often been lost. The original name has perhaps been corrupted out of all recognition, or the careless native of to-day, who is content to take things as they are, has never taken the trouble to ask how they became so. He has been born, and has lived all his life, in the village, and it does not occur to him to suppose that there is any meaning in a name which he hears every day of his life. To him it is just a name, and nothing more. When I asked for an explanation of the name Kuhur, the village of Kuhu, or the Loud Cry, I was told vaguely of some tradition that at the time of its founding a voice from heaven had been mysteriously heard.* The village of Punjai, which, so written, means "dry land," furnishes a good example of the corruption of names. When I arrived at the village, I found only wet fields, and concluded that

* Kuhu, however, appears in "Manu" as the goddess of the new-moon day.

here was another instance of the *lucus a non lucendo.* But the villagers told me that the name was really Pon-cey, or the "golden crow," and related the following legend :—

There is a tank not far from the village, and one day a flock of crows flew over it, pecking to death a sick one among their number. Being now exhausted and at the point of death, the poor crow was dropping into the tank, when the god Siva appeared, scattered its tormentors, and changed the dying crow into gold. In this form it fell into the tank, and gave its name to the village which stands there to-day.

Another instance of the corruption of names is to be found in the word Chicacole. The Telugu name of this, Sri Kakulam, appears to be derived from the name of the presiding deity, but the real explanation is probably that the name consists of two Hindustani words, signifying the opening of parcels. The place is a great Mahometan centre, and was at one time of considerable importance; the name, therefore, probably refers only to the prosaic business of the post.

Every nation, probably, has traditions or superstitions connected with animals. The imagination or philosophy which crowned Athens Queen of Wisdom, and made of the rainbow a goddess with many-coloured wings, sought also to account for the colour of a bird's wing or the eruption of a volcano by romantic theories. The Greeks supposed that the crow was originally white, and that it was changed to black by the anger of Apollo; the peacock in like manner obtaining its beautiful tail from Hera, who, also to punish the importunacy of the bird, endowed it with its discordant voice. Even the more matter-of-fact Roman accepted the auguries of birds which flew on his right hand or his left, and to him the wolf was always sacred, for obvious reasons. We also are not without our superstitions. A crow flying over a house is a presage of evil; it is a sign of good luck if a black cat follows you; while, on the other hand, a black dog is symbolic of the evil one. Amongst the natives the toddy-drawers of the south of India pursue the squirrel with an inveterate hatred, and will kill it when they can, even though the chase be long and wearisome. And this is the cause:—

Once upon a time one of the gods, having compassion on the toddy-drawers because their life was a hard one, and because they were always exposed to danger, left at the foot of a palmyra tree some charmed water, the virtue of which was that it saved from injury any one falling from a height.

The toddy-drawer, however, father of the race, was drunk, and, forgetting to drink the elixir, went home. When he returned he found that a squirrel had drunk it, and vowed vengeance on it. And that is why every toddy-drawer will always kill a squirrel, and also why the squirrel, from whatever height he may fall, comes to no harm.

The squirrel was favoured more than once by the gods. For when Rama was going to Ceylon to rescue Sita from the power of Ravana, he found no means to cross the straits. Thereupon an army of squirrels gathered together, and by wetting their bodies, rolling on the sand, and then shaking themselves, they formed a dam which reached from India to Ceylon. Rama, in gratitude, stroked the squirrel, and, just as men say the breast of the robin was stained with the blood of Christ's feet, as it strove to loosen the nails, so the native thinks that the squirrel still bears the imprint of the god's fingers.

The crow, which sits, like impudence incarnate, with head cocked on one side, and one little eye ever on the watch, has induced in the native mind the belief that it is always blind of one eye. Rama, they say, was one day sleeping by the side of Sita when an asura,* being enamoured of her, descended in the form of a crow and tried to attract her attention. Sita, true to that perfect chastity which all the legends love to extol, took no notice of his blandishments. The asura-crow, however, was not to be denied. He began to peck at her breasts, even drawing blood. At this Rama awoke, and seizing in his rage the nearest weapon, which happened to be a blade of grass, he flung it at the offending crow. The latter begged for mercy, but the weapon of Rama, once it has left his hand, cannot fall ineffectual, and the asura therefore offered one of his eyes as a sacrifice. It would seem, however, that the curse which his weapon inflicted was not the loss of one particular eye, but rather of the power to see out of both eyes at the same time.

This is one of those many stories that Hindus love to tell of the almighty power of Rama, of the chastity of Sita, and of the overthrow of asuras and other evil genii. It seems strange that the crow should thus be made to suffer for the fault of the asura, but every English boy learns that the serpent is doomed to glide upon the ground because Satan once used him as a means to

* Demon.

compass man's fall. The logic in both cases is perhaps at fault, but it is not worse in the one than in the other.

Peculiarly sacred in the eyes of the villagers is the marriage of the masculine banyan to his bride, the fair margosa. Around them they march in solemn procession; and before them men and women pray and vow their vows unto the Lord.

Of the *vráli* bush, which yields no sap, the people have the following belief. The bush had sap once, as other trees have, and its sap had the peculiar power of turning base metals into gold. But the gods, looking down from heaven, and seeing that men were covetous, and that the tree only increased avarice, cursed it for man's sake. And from that time forward it has been dry.

Birds especially, and their peculiarities, seem to have seized upon the Hindu imagination. The white neck feathers of the vulture, the bird of Vishnu, are said to be the garland which the god gave to his favourite, being well pleased with his faithful service. And of this bird they tell also another story. Not more ceaselessly does Philomela bewail the lost Itys than this bird of Vishnu calls ever for Krishna in the vain search for him. For one day Vishnu (who is

Krishna) and his favourite had a contest as to which of the two could more easily detect the hiding-place of the other. Garuda, the vulture, first hid himself, but the all-seeing Krishna discovered him, though only after long search. Then Krishna hid himself in the bird's own eyes; and Garuda to this day is searching for the god, crying incessantly, "Krishna! Krishna! Krishna!" Men say that even now the god may be seen, hiding himself in the pupil of the vulture's eye.

In the land where the cobra is venerated as a god, and where the great Sesha is one of the Hindu hierarchy, one expects to find popular superstitions relating to the serpent. To the Christian mind, brought up to look upon the serpent as the emblem of all evil, the author of the original sin, and the criminal on whom fell the primal curse, the idea of worshipping a snake may seem almost repulsive. But the Hindu sees only its beauty; it is constantly appearing in his legends; it is the emblem of eternity, and it has a subtle, mysterious power of causing swift death. Against that mysterious power the people have a mysterious charm, known only to a few, and guarded jealously by ceremonial rites. For as the witch's herbs had virtue only when gathered by the light of the moon, so this charm cannot be learnt except at certain times of the day. The teacher and the learner must stand waist deep in water, and breast must touch breast. There the mysterious charm is told under oath of strictest secrecy, and to the duly initiated the people flock with the firmest belief in the power of their incantations. The lapse of time which proves the bite innocuous has no effect on this belief; the victim has been bitten by a snake; his imagination throws him into a kind of stupor, and he will walk even miles to the magician, quite unconscious of the fact that, were the snake poisonous, he would be a dead man before he had covered many yards. And the people say of the snake that its tongue was originally as that of other animals. But in the churning of the ocean the gods used the serpent as a rope to draw up the celestial ambrosia. When they had got it, and were sharing it, the serpent licked off a few drops which had fallen on some blades of grass. The grass was sharp-edged and cut the serpent's tongue. And that is the reason why it is forked now.

It is these little things, the smaller traditions in which the people believe, that give us at least a glimpse into their everyday life—that life which they live apart from contact with the European, be he revenue officer, magistrate, or engineer. They will sit for ever listening to the stories of the Puranas, the Ramayana, and the Mahabharata ; but this reveals nothing to us. It is, perhaps, more their love of the marvellous than their religion which impels them to such rapt attention. One does not judge children by their reception of the Bible, for the love of incident is always present. Pharaoh's plagues are more interesting to children than the Decalogue, and Daniel demands more attention as the victim in the lions' den than as the mysterious dreamer of dreams. The tales of the great epics and the sacred books have, therefore, a smaller relative value than the trivial beliefs current among the people, concerning animals and birds and trees.

Such traditions as these have been handed down for generations, not merely among the ruder people, but also among the educated classes. And when we see these things, we cannot but wonder at the stupendous conservatism of the Hindu religion. While they acknowledge the inventions and the methods of the West, they still cling fondly to the superstitions of the East. The judge who to-day gives decisions in accordance with the rules of logic, cures snake-bites to-morrow in all simplicity of unreasoning belief. The merchant, recognizing the value of steamers, eats no food while he is aboard, or, making use of a fraud which deceives no one, prepares his own meal on a little earth brought from the shore. Let him that is without sin first cast a stone at them; for there are not many among us also who do not hold fast in the same unreasoning faith to traditions which, as far as is humanly possible, natural science has demonstrated to be untrue.

But in truth we are not treating of the highly educated class—that class which now and again denies its most sacred traditions from a false idea of keeping up appearances. The town-bred class turned out of our universities with a neat polish of English and the sciences, is not representative of the people of South India. One does not choose as examples of the English people either the members of the Reform Club on the one hand, or, on the other, the proletariat of a London slum. The life of India is not to be sought in the merchants and lawyers of the town or amongst the pariahs and out-castes of the villages. It is in the village community and amongst the respectable farming classes that we must look for those traditions and that folk-lore which are household words to-day. Ask an ignorant toddy-drawer why he pursues a squirrel, and you will perhaps get no reasons in answer; in our own country, though many of its votaries cannot tell you its origin, the Punch-and-Judy show is none the less a national institution. Nor is it to the purpose if some scholar or philologist object that many of the traditions have been drawn from the Puranas or other ancient books. It is difficult to view one's own religion from the standpoint of an impartial judge. We take the religion and its details too much for granted, but Noah and his deluge are surely traditions which live for many, nor is the fact altered because learned men tell us of Hasisadra and his pilot Nes-Hea.

But of all superstitions which a nation can hold, those relating to ghosts are the most interesting as well as the most universal. From the days of the witch of Endor, who called up the spirit of Samuel, to Mr. Sludge, the medium of to-day, there have always been those who believe and tremble, and those who say, with the famous woman, "Je ne les crois pas, mais je les crains." In Greece, where the ghosts of the hundred and ninety-two Athenians slain at Marathon torment the bodies of the merely curious, as well as in Mariner's Friendly Islands, where the *atuas*, or spirits of the departed, return to priests, relations, and others, either in dreams or in the form of apparitions, the belief in spirits exercises a very real influence over the living. The Hindus, as well as the Greeks, furnish the departed spirit with the means for the journey; but such ghosts we may leave to cross Styx in safety, or to wail for ever on the shores of Acheron. Our business lies rather with those malignant spectres whose usual accompaniments are blue lights and clanking chains.

The Hindu ghosts, however, do not, like our English spirits, operate wholly through terror. They do not inhabit houses where some deed of blood has been done. They are not the spirits of retribution, called up by the conscience of the murderer. They are spectres of pure malignancy—horrid ghouls, who lurk invisible by day and night about the houses of the peasants, listening for news which will give them a chance to decoy, to terrify, and to murder. By night, too, they roam about in the jungles, in the thickets, and in lonely places, avoiding, as far as possible, the villages and the habitations of man. A woman perhaps arranges to go out early in the morning with a companion, to gather sticks, it may be, or for some other household purpose. If a ghost hears their conversation, he puts on the form of one of the women, and goes at dead of night to the house of the other, taps at the door, and calls her, saying it is near daybreak and time to start. The poor woman goes out unsuspectingly, but she never returns, for once they are well clear of the village, the ghost turns upon her and kills her. Women, therefore, if they have to go out early in the morning, make their arrangements in the daytime and in their houses, for fear of ghosts. For ghosts, like all evil things, love the darkness, and when you are out of doors you never know that one or two listening spirits of mischief are not at your elbow.

But cunning as the ghosts may be in getting their information and in deceiving unsuspecting women, they are themselves outwitted by very simple tricks. A woman who was decoyed into the plain on the pretext of gathering fuel, discovered that her companion was a spectre. So she pretended to lie down and go to sleep, covering herself up with a cloth. Meanwhile the ghost went on gathering sticks, and the woman, quietly substituting her basket for herself, slipped away home. When the time came for the murder, the ghost of course found out that his victim had disappeared, and in his rage at being tricked he tore the basket to pieces.

These spirits, it seems, are like wild men, with tangled hair hanging about their faces; but they are always easily distinguished from human beings, for they have *no legs*. One is surprised that with this glaring defect they can ever deceive any one; but ghost stories do not always bear close examination, and we know how difficult it is to find any one who has himself seen a ghost. Probably the best authority in the village is only some one who heard from some one else that a friend of his had seen something uncanny.

In the middle of the night these horrid goblins assemble at some grove outside the village, and there they hold their ghoulish revel, dancing their *danses macabres,* singing their weird songs, or playing games, perhaps with human skulls. Some sit round their ghostly fire, telling many tales of strangled children and women done to death, and one will show a finger and another an ear, torn from the corpses of their victims. A man, it is said, once visited this hall of the ghosts, to get back his wife's necklace, which they had stolen. He disguised himself as a ghost, by letting his hair fall over his face, and joined in the dance! The necklace was passed from one to the other, and when it came to the man he slipped away, unobserved by the dancing ghosts! We are not told what he did with his tell-tale legs—but, after all, ghosts are very simple creatures!

But there is one thing of which ghosts stand in special awe, and that is iron. Shepherds, therefore, the robber castes, and others, whose business calls them out of the village at night, always carry about iron in some shape or other. Many wear an iron finger- or toe-ring as a talisman. Such is the power of iron, that ghosts are not only terrified at sight of it, but may even be reduced to servitude by it. One of them, which was captured by a charmer, was thus kept in bondage by a nail driven into its head (for ghosts do not feel), and did the work of a domestic servant for years. But one day, after it had dressed the hair of the ladies, it asked a young girl to comb its hair for it. While the girl was doing this she came across the nail. The ghost asked her to take it out, and she, suspecting nothing, did so. No sooner was the nail out than the charm was broken, and the ghost, being thus set at liberty, ran away.

Such superstitions are very present realities to the people of the villages. It matters little to them that they are in many cases demonstrably false. The year Vikari (called 1899 of the Christian era) was to be a year of calamity. Seven planets, it is said, then met in one sign of the zodiac. This heralded the end of the world. The tenth avatar of Vishnu was to be made manifest; the god was to appear, mounted on a white horse, armed with a scimitar, and blazing like a comet. The world with all its wickedness was to be burnt up and a new age of purity was to begin. But the steadfast earth remains, and the day seems still far off when the heavens shall pass away with a great noise, and the elements shall melt with fervent heat.

And the placid life of the villagers continues. They know nothing of history, and do not care to know; the sound of wars that stir up the hearts of Western nations never reaches their ears; the laws and the government suffer change, but the traditions remain, deep fixed in the hearts of the most conservative of peoples, and upheld by the most self-contained of religions.

THE END.

A Classified Catalogue

OF WORKS IN

GENERAL LITERATURE

PUBLISHED BY

LONGMANS, GREEN, & CO.

39 PATERNOSTER ROW, LONDON, E.C.

91 AND 93 FIFTH AVENUE, NEW YORK, AND 32 HORNBY ROAD, BOMBAY.

CONTENTS.

INDEX OF AUTHORS AND EDITORS.

INDEX OF AUTHORS AND EDITORS—*continued.*

History, Politics, Polity, Political Memoirs, &c.

Abbott.—*A History of Greece.* By Evelyn Abbott, M.A., LL.D.

Part I.—From the Earliest Times to the Ionian Revolt. Crown 8vo., 10s. 6d.

Part II.—500-445 B.C. Crown 8vo., 10s. 6d.

Part III.—From the Peace of 445 B.C. to the Fall of the Thirty at Athens in 403 B.C. Crown 8vo., 10s. 6d.

Acland and Ransome.—*A Handbook in Outline of the Political History of England to* 1896. Chronologically Arranged. By the Right Hon. A. H. Dyke Acland, and Cyril Ransome, M.A. Crown 8vo., 6s.

Amos.—*Primer of the English Constitution and Government.* For the Use of Colleges, Schools, and Private Students. By Sheldon Amos, M.A. Cr. 8vo., 6s.

Annual Register (The). A Review of Public Events at Home and Abroad, for the year 1899. 8vo., 18s.

Volumes of the *Annual Register* for the years 1863-1898 can still be had. 18s. each.

Arnold.—*Introductory Lectures on Modern History.* By Thomas Arnold, D.D., formerly Head Master of Rugby School. 8vo., 7s. 6d.

Ashbourne.—*Pitt: Some Chapters on His Life and Times.* By the Right Hon. Edward Gibson, Lord Ashbourne, Lord Chancellor of Ireland. With 11 Portraits. 8vo., 21s.

Ashley.—*Surveys, Historic and Economic:* a Volume of Essays. By W. J. Ashley, M.A. 8vo., 9s. net.

Baden-Powell.—*The Indian Village Community.* Examined with Reference to the Physical, Ethnographic, and Historical Conditions of the Provinces; chiefly on the Basis of the Revenue-Settlement Records and District Manuals. By B. H. Baden-Powell, M.A., C.I.E. With Map. 8vo., 16s.

Bagwell.—*Ireland under the Tudors.* By Richard Bagwell, LL.D. (3 vols.) Vols. I. and II. From the first invasion of the Northmen to the year 1578. 8vo., 32s. Vol. III. 1578-1603. 8vo., 18s.

Besant.—*The History of London.* By Sir Walter Besant. With 74 Illustrations. Crown 8vo., 1s. 9d. Or bound as a School Prize Book, 2s. 6d.

Bright.—*A History of England.* By the Rev. J. Franck Bright, D.D.

Period I. *Mediæval Monarchy:* A.D. 449-1485. Crown 8vo., 4s. 6d.

Period II. *Personal Monarchy.* 1485-1688. Crown 8vo., 5s.

Period III. *Constitutional Monarchy.* 1689-1837. Crown 8vo., 7s. 6d.

Period IV. *The Growth of Democracy.* 1837-1880. Crown 8vo., 6s.

Bruce.—*The Forward Policy and its Results;* or, Thirty-five Years' Work amongst the Tribes on our North-Western Frontier of India. By Richard Isaac Bruce, C.I.E. With 28 Illustrations and a Map. 8vo., 15s. net.

Buckle.—*History of Civilisation in England, France, Spain, and Scotland.* By Henry Thomas Buckle. 3 vols. Crown 8vo., 24s.

Burke.—*A History of Spain, from the Earliest Times to the Death of Ferdinand the Catholic.* By Ulick Ralph Burke, M.A. Edited by Martin A. S. Hume. With 6 Maps. 2 vols. Crown 8vo., 16s. net.

Chesney.—*Indian Polity:* a View of the System of Administration in India. By General Sir George Chesney, K.C.B. With Map showing all the Administrative Divisions of British India. 8vo., 21s.

Churchill (Winston Spencer, M.P.).

The River War: an Historical Account of the Reconquest of the Soudan. Edited by Colonel F. Rhodes, D.S.O. With 34 Maps and 51 Illustrations, also 7 Portraits. 2 vols. Medium 8vo., 36s.

The Story of the Malakand Field Force, 1897. With 6 Maps and Plans. Crown 8vo., 3s. 6d.

London to Ladysmith viâ Pretoria. With 3 Folding-out Maps and 1 Map and 4 Plans in the Text. Crown 8vo., 6s.

Ian Hamilton's March. With Portrait of Lieut.-General Ian Hamilton, and 10 Maps and Plans. Crown 8vo., 6s.

History, Politics, Polity, Political Memoirs, &c.—*continued.*

Corbett (JULIAN S.).

DRAKE AND THE TUDOR NAVY, with a History of the Rise of England as a Maritime Power. With Portraits, Illustrations and Maps. 2 vols. Crown 8vo., 16*s.*

THE SUCCESSORS OF DRAKE. With 4 Portraits (2 Photogravures) and 12 Maps and Plans. 8vo., 21*s.*

Creighton (M., D.D., Lord Bishop of London).

A HISTORY OF THE PAPACY FROM THE GREAT SCHISM TO THE SACK OF ROME, 1378-1527. 6 vols. Cr. 8vo., 6*s.* each.

QUEEN ELIZABETH. With Portrait. Crown 8vo., 6*s.*

Curzon.—*PERSIA AND THE PERSIAN QUESTION.* By the Right Hon. LORD CURZON OF KEDLESTON. With 9 Maps, 96 Illustrations, Appendices, and an Index. 2 vols. 8vo., 42*s.*

De Tocqueville.—*DEMOCRACY IN AMERICA.* By ALEXIS DE TOCQUEVILLE. Translated by HENRY REEVE, C.B., D.C.L. 2 vols. Crown 8vo., 16*s.*

Dickinson.—*THE DEVELOPMENT OF PARLIAMENT DURING THE NINETEENTH CENTURY.* By G. LOWES DICKINSON, M.A. 8vo., 7*s.* 6*d.*

Froude (JAMES A.).

THE HISTORY OF ENGLAND, from the Fall of Wolsey to the Defeat of the Spanish Armada. 12 vols. Crown 8vo., 3*s.* 6*d.* each.

THE DIVORCE OF CATHERINE OF ARAGON. Crown 8vo., 3*s.* 6*d.*

THE SPANISH STORY OF THE ARMADA, and other Essays. Cr. 8vo., 3*s.* 6*d.*

THE ENGLISH IN IRELAND IN THE EIGHTEENTH CENTURY. 3 vols. Cr. 8vo., 10*s.* 6*d.*

ENGLISH SEAMEN IN THE SIXTEENTH CENTURY. Cr. 8vo., 6*s.*

THE COUNCIL OF TRENT. Crown 8vo., 3*s.* 6*d.*

SHORT STUDIES ON GREAT SUBJECTS. 4 vols. Cr. 8vo., 3*s.* 6*d.* each.

CÆSAR: a Sketch. Cr. 8vo, 3*s.* 6*d.*

Gardiner (SAMUEL RAWSON, D.C.L., LL.D.).

HISTORY OF ENGLAND, from the Accession of James I. to the Outbreak of the Civil War, 1603-1642. 10 vols. Crown 8vo., 6*s.* each.

A HISTORY OF THE GREAT CIVIL WAR, 1642-1649. 4 vols. Cr. 8vo., 6*s.* each.

A HISTORY OF THE COMMONWEALTH AND THE PROTECTORATE. 1649-1660. Vol. I. 1649-1651. With 14 Maps. 8vo., 21*s.* Vol. II. 1651-1654. With 7 Maps. 8vo., 21*s.*

WHAT GUNPOWDER PLOT WAS. With 8 Illustrations. Crown 8vo., 5*s.*

CROMWELL'S PLACE IN HISTORY. Founded on Six Lectures delivered in the University of Oxford. Cr. 8vo., 3*s.* 6*d.*

THE STUDENT'S HISTORY OF ENGLAND. With 378 Illustrations. Crown 8vo., 12*s.*

Also in Three Volumes, price 4*s.* each.

Vol. I. B.C. 55—A.D. 1509. 173 Illustrations.
Vol. II. 1509-1689. 96 Illustrations.
Vol. III. 1689-1885. 109 Illustrations.

Greville.—*A JOURNAL OF THE REIGNS OF KING GEORGE IV., KING WILLIAM IV., AND QUEEN VICTORIA.* By CHARLES C. F. GREVILLE, formerly Clerk of the Council. 8 vols. Crown 8vo., 3*s.* 6*d.* each.

Gross.—*THE SOURCES AND LITERATURE OF ENGLISH HISTORY, FROM THE EARLIEST TIMES TO ABOUT* 1485. By CHARLES GROSS, Ph.D. 8vo.

Hammond.—*A WOMAN'S PART IN A REVOLUTION.* By Mrs. JOHN HAYS HAMMOND. Crown 8vo., 2*s.* 6*d.*

Historic Towns.—Edited by E. A. FREEMAN, D.C.L., and Rev. WILLIAM HUNT, M.A. With Maps and Plans. Crown 8vo., 3*s.* 6*d.* each.

Bristol. By Rev. W. Hunt.
Carlisle. By Mandell Creighton, D.D.
Cinque Ports. By Montagu Burrows.
Colchester. By Rev. E. L. Cutts.
Exeter. By E. A. Freeman.
London. By Rev. W. J. Loftie.
Oxford. By Rev. C. W. Boase.
Winchester. By G. W. Kitchin, D.D.
York. By Rev. James Raine.
New York. By Theodore Roosevelt.
Boston (U.S.) By Henry Cabot Lodge.

History, Politics, Polity, Political Memoirs, &c.—*continued.*

HARVARD HISTORICAL STUDIES.

THE SUPPRESSION OF THE AFRICAN SLAVE TRADE TO THE UNITED STATES OF AMERICA, 1638-1870. By W. E. B. DU BOIS, Ph.D. 8vo., 7s. 6d.

THE CONTEST OVER THE RATIFICATON OF THE FEDERAL CONSTITUTION IN MASSACHUSETTS. By S. B. HARDING, A.M. 8vo., 6s.

A CRITICAL STUDY OF NULLIFICATION IN SOUTH CAROLINA. By D. F. HOUSTON, A.M. 8vo., 6s.

NOMINATIONS FOR ELECTIVE OFFICE IN THE UNITED STATES. By FREDERICK W. DALLINGER, A.M. 8vo., 7s. 6d.

A BIBLIOGRAPHY OF BRITISH MUNICIPAL HISTORY, INCLUDING GILDS AND PARLIAMENTARY REPRESENTATION. By CHARLES GROSS, Ph.D. 8vo., 12s.

THE LIBERTY AND FREE SOIL PARTIES IN THE NORTH WEST. By THEODORE C. SMITH, Ph.D. 8vo, 7s. 6d.

THE PROVINCIAL GOVERNOR IN THE ENGLISH COLONIES OF NORTH AMERICA. By EVARTS BOUTELL GREENE. 8vo., 7s. 6d.

THE COUNTY PALATINE OF DURHAM: a Study in Constitutional History. By GAILLARD THOMAS LAPSLEY, Ph.D. 8vo., 10s. 6d.

*** *Other Volumes are in preparation.*

Hunter.—*A HISTORY OF BRITISH INDIA.* By Sir WILLIAM WILSON HUNTER, K.C.S.I., M.A., LL.D. Vol. I. Introductory to the Overthrow of the English in the Spice Archipelago, 1623. With 4 Maps. 8vo., 18s. Vol. II.—To the Union of the Old and New Companies under the Earl of Godolphin's Award, 1708. 8vo., 16s.

Ingram.—*A CRITICAL EXAMINATION OF IRISH HISTORY:* being a Replacement of the False by the True. From the Elizabethan Conquest to the Legislative Union of 1800. By T. DUNBAR INGRAM, LL.D. 2 vols. 8vo.

Joyce (P. W., LL.D.).

A SHORT HISTORY OF IRELAND, from the Earliest Times to 1603. Crown 8vo., 10s. 6d.

A CHILD'S HISTORY OF IRELAND. From the Earliest Times to the Death of O'Connell. With specially constructed Map and 160 Illustrations, including Facsimile in full colours of an illuminated page of the Gospel Book of MacDurnan, A.D. 850. Fcp. 8vo., 3s. 6d.

Kaye and Malleson.—*HISTORY OF THE INDIAN MUTINY*, 1857-1858. By Sir JOHN W. KAYE and Colonel G. B. MALLESON. With Analytical Index and Maps and Plans. 6 vols. Crown 8vo., 3s. 6d. each.

Kent.—*THE ENGLISH RADICALS:* an Historical Sketch. By C. B. ROYLANCE KENT. Crown 8vo., 7s. 6d.

Lang.—*THE COMPANIONS OF PICKLE:* Being a Sequel to 'Pickle the Spy'. By ANDREW LANG. With 4 Plates. 8vo., 16s.

Laurie.—*HISTORICAL SURVEY OF PRE-CHRISTIAN EDUCATION.* By S. S. LAURIE, A.M., LL.D. Crown 8vo., 7s. 6d.

Lecky (The Rt. Hon. WILLIAM E. H.)

HISTORY OF ENGLAND IN THE EIGHTEENTH CENTURY.

Library Edition. 8 vols. 8vo. Vols. I. and II., 1700-1760, 36s.; Vols. III. and IV., 1760-1784, 36s.; Vols. V. and VI., 1784-1793, 36s.; Vols. VII. and VIII., 1793-1800, 36s.

Cabinet Edition. ENGLAND. 7 vols. Crown 8vo., 6s. each. IRELAND. 5 vols. Crown 8vo., 6s. each.

HISTORY OF EUROPEAN MORALS FROM AUGUSTUS TO CHARLEMAGNE. 2 vols. Crown 8vo., 12s.

HISTORY OF THE RISE AND INFLUENCE OF THE SPIRIT OF RATIONALISM IN EUROPE. 2 vols. Crown 8vo., 12s.

DEMOCRACY AND LIBERTY.

Library Edition. 2 vols. 8vo., 36s.

Cabinet Edition. 2 vols. Cr. 8vo., 12s.

Lowell.—*GOVERNMENTS AND PARTIES IN CONTINENTAL EUROPE.* By A. LAWRENCE LOWELL. 2 vols. 8vo., 21s.

Lytton. *THE HISTORY OF LORD LYTTON'S INDIAN ADMINISTRATION, FROM* 1876-1880. Compiled from Letters and Official Papers. Edited by Lady BETTY BALFOUR. With Portrait and Map. 8vo., 18s.

History, Politics, Polity, Political Memoirs, &c.—*continued.*

Macaulay (Lord).

Complete Works.

'Albany' Edition. With 12 Portraits. 12 vols. Large Crown 8vo., 3s. 6d. each.

'Edinburgh' Edition. 8 vols. 8vo., 6s. each.

Cabinet Edition. 16 vols. Post 8vo., £4 16s.

History of England from the Accession of James the Second.
Popular Edition. 2 vols. Cr. 8vo., 5s.
Student's Edition. 2 vols. Cr. 8vo., 12s.
People's Edition. 4 vols. Cr. 8vo., 16s.
'Albany' Edition. With 6 Portraits. 6 vols. Large Crown 8vo., 3s. 6d. each.
Cabinet Edition. 8 vols. Post 8vo., 48s.
'Edinburgh' Edition. 4 vols. 8vo., 6s. each.
Library Edition. 5 vols. 8vo., £4.

Critical and Historical Essays, with Lays of Ancient Rome, etc., in 1 volume.
Popular Edition. Crown 8vo., 2s. 6d.
Authorised Edition. Crown 8vo., 2s. 6d., or gilt edges, 3s. 6d.
'Silver Library' Edition. With Portrait and 4 Illustrations to the 'Lays'. Cr. 8vo., 3s. 6d.

Critical and Historical Essays.
Student's Edition. 1 vol. Cr. 8vo., 6s.
People's Edition. 2 vols. Cr. 8vo., 8s.
'Trevelyan' Edition. 2 vols. Cr. 8vo., 9s.
Cabinet Edition. 4 vols. Post 8vo., 24s.
'Edinburgh' Edition. 3 vols. 8vo., 6s. each.
Library Edition. 3 vols. 8vo., 36s.

Essays, which may be had separately, sewed, 6d. each; cloth, 1s. each.

Addison and Walpole.
Croker's Boswell's Johnson.
Hallam's Constitutional History.
Warren Hastings.
The Earl of Chatham (Two Essays).
Frederick the Great.
Ranke and Gladstone.
Lord Bacon.
Lord Clive.
Lord Byron, and The Comic Dramatists of the Restoration.

Miscellaneous Writings.
People's Edition. 1 vol. Cr. 8vo., 4s. 6d.
Library Edition. 2 vols. 8vo., 21s.

Miscellaneous Writings, Speeches and Poems.
Popular Edition. Crown 8vo., 2s. 6d.
Cabinet Edition. 4 vols. Post 8vo., 24s.

Selections from the Writings of Lord Macaulay. Edited, with Occasional Notes, by the Right Hon. Sir G. O. Trevelyan, Bart. Crown 8vo., 6s.

Mackinnon.—*The History of Edward the Third.* By James Mackinnon, Ph.D., Lecturer on History in the University of St. Andrews. 8vo., 18s.

May.—*The Constitutional History of England* since the Accession of George III. 1760-1870. By Sir Thomas Erskine May, K.C.B. (Lord Farnborough). 3 vols. Cr. 8vo., 18s.

Merivale (Charles, D.D.).

History of the Romans under the Empire. 8 vols. Crown 8vo., 3s. 6d. each.

The Fall of the Roman Republic: a Short History of the Last Century of the Commonwealth. 12mo., 7s. 6d.

General History of Rome, from the Foundation of the City to the Fall of Augustulus, B.C. 753-A.D. 476. With 5 Maps. Crown 8vo, 7s. 6d.

Montague. — *The Elements of English Constitutional History.* By F. C. Montague, M.A. Crown 8vo., 3s. 6d.

Phillips.—*South African Recollections.* By Florence Phillips (Mrs. Lionel Phillips). With 37 Illustrations from Photographs. 8vo., 7s. 6d.

Powell and Trevelyan. — *The Peasants' Rising and the Lollards:* a Collection of Unpublished Documents, forming an Appendix to 'England in the Age of Wycliffe'. Edited by Edgar Powell and G. M. Trevelyan. 8vo., 6s. net.

Ransome.—*The Rise of Constitutional Government in England.* By Cyril Ransome, M.A. Crown 8vo., 6s.

Seebohm.—*The English Village Community* Examined in its Relations to the Manorial and Tribal Systems, etc. By Frederic Seebohm, LL.D., F.S.A. With 13 Maps and Plates. 8vo., 16s.

Shaw.—*A History of the English Church during the Civil Wars and under the Commonwealth*, 1640-1660. By William A. Shaw, Litt.D. 2 vols. 8vo., 36s.

Smith.—*Carthage and the Carthaginians.* By R. Bosworth Smith, M.A., With Maps, Plans, etc. Cr. 8vo., 3s. 6d.

Stephens. — *A History of the French Revolution.* By H. Morse Stephens. 8vo. Vols. I. and II. 18s. each.

Stubbs.—*History of the University of Dublin*, from its Foundation to the End of the Eighteenth Century. By J. W. Stubbs. 8vo., 12s. 6d.

History, Politics, Polity, Political Memoirs, &c.—*continued.*

Sutherland.—*The History of Australia and New Zealand*, from 1606-1890. By Alexander Sutherland, M.A., and George Sutherland, M.A. Crown 8vo., 2s. 6d.

Taylor.—*A Student's Manual of the History of India.* By Colonel Meadows Taylor, C.S.I., etc. Cr. 8vo., 7s. 6d.

Todd.—*Parliamentary Government in the British Colonies.* By Alpheus Todd, LL.D. 8vo., 30s. net.

Trevelyan.—*The American Revolution.* Part I. 1766-1776. By the Rt. Hon. Sir G. O. Trevelyan, Bart. 8vo., 16s.

Trevelyan.—*England in the Age of Wycliffe.* By George Macaulay Trevelyan. 8vo., 15s.

Wakeman and Hassall.—*Essays Introductory to the Study of English Constitutional History.* Edited by Henry Offley Wakeman, M.A., and Arthur Hassall, M.A. Crown 8vo., 6s.

Walpole.—*History of England from the Conclusion of the Great War in 1815 to 1858.* By Sir Spencer Walpole, K.C.B. 6 vols. Cr. 8vo., 6s. each.

Wood-Martin.—*Pagan Ireland: an Archæological Sketch.* A Handbook of Irish Pre-Christian Antiquities. By W. G. Wood-Martin, M.R.I.A. With 512 Illustrations. Crown 8vo., 15s.

Wylie (James Hamilton, M.A.).

History of England under Henry IV. 4 vols. Crown 8vo. Vol. I., 1399-1404, 10s. 6d. Vol. II., 1405-1406, 15s. (*out of print*). Vol. III., 1407-1411, 15s. Vol. IV., 1411-1413, 21s.

The Council of Constance to the Death of John Hus: Being the Ford Lectures delivered in the University of Oxford in Lent Term, 1900. Crown 8vo., 6s. net.

Biography, Personal Memoirs, &c.

Bacon.—*The Letters and Life of Francis Bacon, including all his Occasional Works.* Edited by James Spedding. 7 vols. 8vo., £4 4s.

Bagehot.—*Biographical Studies.* By Walter Bagehot. Crown 8vo., 3s. 6d.

Carlyle.—*Thomas Carlyle:* A History of his Life. By James Anthony Froude.

1795-1835. 2 vols. Crown 8vo., 7s.
1834-1881. 2 vols. Crown 8vo., 7s.

Cellini.—*Chisel, Pen, and Poignard;* or, Benvenuto Cellini, his Times and his Contemporaries. By the Author of 'The Life of Sir Kenelm Digby,' 'The Life of a Prig,' etc. With 19 Illustrations. Crown 8vo., 5s.

Crozier.—*My Inner Life:* being a Chapter in Personal Evolution and Autobiography. By John Beattie Crozier, Author of 'Civilisation and Progress,' etc. 8vo., 14s.

Dante.—*The Life and Works of Dante Allighieri:* being an Introduction to the Study of the 'Divina Commedia'. By the Rev. J. F. Hogan, D.D., Professor, St. Patrick's College, Maynooth. With Portrait. 8vo., 12s. 6d.

Danton.—*Life of Danton.* By A. H. Beesly. With Portraits of Danton, his Mother, and an Illustration of the Home of his family at Arcis. Crown 8vo., 6s.

De Bode.—*The Baroness de Bode,* 1775-1803: being a Chronicle of the Strange Experiences of an English Lady, Wife of a German Baron possessed of a Fief in Alsace, during the French Revolution, afterwards an Immigrant in Russia. By William S. Childe-Pemberton. With 4 Photogravure Portraits and other Illustrations. 8vo., 12s. 6d. net.

Douglass.—*Life of Sir James Nicholas Douglass, F.R.S., etc.,* formerly Engineer-in-Chief to the Trinity House. By Thomas Williams. With Portrait. Crown 8vo., 3s. 6d.

Duncan.—*Admiral Duncan.* By The Earl of Camperdown. With 3 Portraits. 8vo., 16s.

Erasmus.—*Life and Letters of Erasmus.* By James Anthony Froude. Crown 8vo., 3s. 6d.

Faraday.—*Faraday as a Discoverer.* By John Tyndall. Crown 8vo, 3s. 6d.

Foreign Courts and Foreign Homes. By A. M. F. Crown 8vo., 6s.

Fox.—*The Early History of Charles James Fox.* By the Right Hon. Sir G. O. Trevelyan, Bart.

Library Edition. 8vo., 18s.
Cheap Edition. Crown 8vo., 3s. 6d.

Halifax.—*The Life and Letters of Sir George Savile, Baronet, First Marquis of Halifax.* By H. C. Foxcroft. 2 vols. 8vo., 36s.

Biography, Personal Memoirs, &c.—*continued.*

Hamilton.—*LIFE OF SIR WILLIAM HAMILTON.* By R. P. GRAVES. 8vo. 3 vols. 15*s.* each. ADDENDUM. 8vo., 6*d.* sewed.

Havelock.—*MEMOIRS OF SIR HENRY HAVELOCK, K.C.B.* By JOHN CLARK MARSHMAN. Crown 8vo., 3*s.* 6*d.*

Haweis.—*MY MUSICAL LIFE.* By the Rev. H. R. HAWEIS. With Portrait of Richard Wagner and 3 Illustrations. Crown 8vo., 6s. net.

Hiley.—*MEMORIES OF HALF A CENTURY.* By the Rev. R. W. HILEY, D.D., Vicar of Wighill, Tadcaster. With Portrait. 8vo., 15*s.*

Jackson.—*STONEWALL JACKSON AND THE AMERICAN CIVIL WAR.* By Lieut.-Col. G. F. R. HENDERSON. With 2 Portraits and 33 Maps and Plans. 2 vols. Crown 8vo., 16*s.* net.

Leslie.—*THE LIFE AND CAMPAIGNS OF ALEXANDER LESLIE, FIRST EARL OF LEVEN.* By CHARLES SANFORD TERRY, M.A. With Maps and Plans. 8vo., 16s.

Luther.—*LIFE OF LUTHER.* By JULIUS KÖSTLIN. With 62 Illustrations and 4 Facsimilies of MSS. Cr. 8vo., 3*s.* 6*d.*

Macaulay.—*THE LIFE AND LETTERS OF LORD MACAULAY.* By the Right Hon. Sir G. O. TREVELYAN, Bart.

Popular Edition. 1 vol. Cr. 8vo., 2*s.* 6*d.*
Student's Edition 1 vol. Cr. 8vo., 6*s.*
Cabinet Edition. 2 vols. Post 8vo., 12*s.*
'Edinburgh' Edition. 2 vols. 8vo., 6*s.* each
Library Edition. 2 vols. 8vo., 36*s.*

Marbot.—*THE MEMOIRS OF THE BARON DE MARBOT.* Translated from the French. 2 vols. Crown 8vo., 7*s.*

Martineau.—*JAMES MARTINEAU: a Biography and Study.* By A. W. JACKSON, A.M. With 2 Portraits. 8vo., 12*s.* 6*d.*

Max Müller.—*AULD LANG SYNE.* By the Right Hon. F. MAX MÜLLER. First Series. With Portrait. 8vo, 10*s.* 6*d.*

CONTENTS.—Musical Recollections—Literary Recollections—Recollections of Royalties—Beggars.

Second Series. *MY INDIAN FRIENDS.* 8vo, 10*s.* 6*d.*

Morris.—*THE LIFE OF WILLIAM MORRIS.* By J. W. MACKAIL. With 6 Portraits and 16 Illustrations by E. H. NEW. etc. 2 vols. 8vo., 32*s.*

On the Banks of the Seine. By A. M. F. Crown 8vo., 6*s.*

Pearson.—*CHARLES HENRY PEARSON, FELLOW OF ORIEL, AND EDUCATION MINISTER IN VICTORIA;* Author of 'National Life and Character'. Memorials by Himself, his Wife, and his Friends. Edited by W. STEBBING, Hon. Fellow of Worcester College, Oxford. With Portrait. 8vo., 14*s.*

Place.—*THE LIFE OF FRANCIS PLACE, 1771-1854.* By GRAHAM WALLAS, M.A. With 2 Portraits. 8vo., 12*s.*

Râmakrishna: *HIS LIFE AND SAYINGS.* By the Right Hon. F. MAX MÜLLER. Crown 8vo., 5*s.*

Russell.—*SWALLOWFIELD AND ITS OWNERS.* By CONSTANCE LADY RUSSELL, of Swallowfield Park. With Photogravure Portraits and other Illustrations. 4to.

Romanes.—*THE LIFE AND LETTERS OF GEORGE JOHN ROMANES, M.A., LL.D., F.R.S.* Written and Edited by his WIFE. With Portrait and 2 Illustrations. Cr. 8vo., 6*s.*

Seebohm.—*THE OXFORD REFORMERS—JOHN COLET, ERASMUS, AND THOMAS MORE:* a History of their Fellow-Work. By FREDERIC SEEBOHM. 8vo., 14*s.*

Shakespeare.—*OUTLINES OF THE LIFE OF SHAKESPEARE.* By J. O. HALLIWELL-PHILLIPPS. With Illustrations and Fac-similes. 2 vols. Royal 8vo., 21*s.*

Shakespeare's *TRUE LIFE.* By JAMES WALTER With 500 Illustrations by GERALD E. MOIRA. Imp. 8vo., 21*s.* net.

Stanley (Lady).

THE GIRLHOOD OF MARIA JOSEPHA HOLROYD (Lady Stanley of Alderley). Recorded in Letters of a Hundred Years Ago, from 1776-1796. Edited by J. H. ADEANE. With 6 Portraits. 8vo., 18*s.*

THE EARLY MARRIED LIFE OF MARIA JOSEPHA, LADY STANLEY, FROM 1796. Edited by J. H. ADEANE. With 10 Portraits and 3 Illustrations. 8vo., 18*s.*

Verney.—*MEMOIRS OF THE VERNEY FAMILY.* Compiled from the Letters and Illustrated by the Portraits at Clayden House.

Vols. I. & II., *DURING THE CIVIL WAR.* By FRANCES PARTHENOPE VERNEY. With 38 Portraits, etc. Royal 8vo., 42*s.*

Vol. III., *DURING THE COMMONWEALTH. 1650-1660.* By MARGARET M. VERNEY. With 10 Portraits, etc. Royal 8vo., 21*s.*

Vol. IV., *FROM THE RESTORATION TO THE REVOLUTION.* 1660 to 1696. By MARGARET M. VERNEY. With 11 Portraits, etc. Royal 8vo., 21*s.*

Victoria.—*QUEEN VICTORIA, 1819-1900.* By RICHARD R. HOLMES, M.V.O., F.S.A., Librarian to the Queen. With Photogravure Portrait. Crown 8vo., 6*s.*

Wellington.—*LIFE OF THE DUKE OF WELLINGTON.* By the Rev. G. R. GLEIG, M.A. Crown 8vo., 3*s.* 6*d.*

Travel and Adventure, the Colonies, &c.

Arnold.—*Seas and Lands.* By Sir Edwin Arnold. With 71 Illustrations. Crown 8vo., 3*s*. 6*d*.

Ball (John).

The Alpine Guide. Reconstructed and Revised on behalf of the Alpine Club, by W. A. B. Coolidge.

Vol. I., *The Western Alps:* the Alpine Region, South of the Rhone Valley, from the Col de Tenda to the Simplon Pass. With 9 New and Revised Maps. Crown 8vo., 12*s*. net.

Hints and Notes, Practical and Scientific, for Travellers in the Alps: being a Revision of the General Introduction to the 'Alpine Guide'. Crown 8vo., 3*s*. net.

Baker (Sir S. W.).

Eight Years in Ceylon. With 6 Illustrations. Crown 8vo., 3*s*. 6*d*.

The Rifle and the Hound in Ceylon. With 6 Illustrations. Crown 8vo., 3*s*. 6*d*.

Bent.—*The Ruined Cities of Mashonaland:* being a Record of Excavation and Exploration in 1891. By J. Theodore Bent. With 117 Illustrations. Crown 8vo., 3*s*. 6*d*.

Brassey (the late Lady).

A Voyage in the 'Sunbeam'; Our Home on the Ocean for Eleven Months.

Cabinet Edition. With Map and 66 Illustrations. Crown 8vo., 7*s*. 6*d*.
'Silver Library' Edition. With 66 Illustrations. Crown 8vo., 3*s*. 6*d*.
Popular Edition. With 60 Illustrations. 4to., 6*d*. sewed, 1*s*. cloth.
School Edition. With 37 Illustrations. Fcp., 2*s*. cloth, or 3*s*. white parchment.

Sunshine and Storm in the East.
Cabinet Edition. With 2 Maps and 114 Illustrations. Crown 8vo., 7*s*. 6*d*.
Popular Edition. With 103 Illustrations. 4to., 6*d*. sewed, 1*s*. cloth.

In the Trades, the Tropics, and the 'Roaring Forties'.

Cabinet Edition. With Map and 220 Illustrations. Crown 8vo., 7*s*. 6*d*.

Browning.—*A Girl's Wanderings in Hungary.* By H. Ellen Browning. With Map and 20 Illustrations. Crown 8vo., 3*s*. 6*d*.

Froude (James A.).

Oceana: or England and her Colonies. With 9 Illustrations. Cr. 8vo., 3*s*. 6*d*.

The English in the West Indies: or, the Bow of Ulysses. With 9 Illustrations. Crown 8vo., 2*s*. boards, 2*s*. 6*d*. cloth.

Heathcote.—*St. Kilda.* By Norman Heathcote. With 80 Illustrations from Sketches and Photographs of the People, Scenery and Birds by the Author. 8vo., 10*s*. 6*d*. net.

Howitt.—*Visits to Remarkable Places.* Old Halls, Battle-Fields, Scenes, illustrative of Striking Passages in English History and Poetry. By William Howitt. With 80 Illustrations. Crown 8vo., 3*s*. 6*d*.

Knight (E. F.).

The Cruise of the 'Alerte': the Narrative of a Search for Treasure on the Desert Island of Trinidad. With 2 Maps and 23 Illustrations. Crown 8vo., 3*s*. 6*d*.

Where Three Empires meet: a Narrative of Recent Travel in Kashmir, Western Tibet, Baltistan, Ladak, Gilgit, and the adjoining Countries. With a Map and 54 Illustrations. Cr. 8vo., 3*s*. 6*d*.

The 'Falcon' on the Baltic: a Voyage from London to Copenhagen in a Three-Tonner. With 10 Full-page Illustrations. Crown 8vo., 3*s*. 6*d*.

Lees.—*Peaks and Pines:* another Norway Book. By J. A. Lees. With 63 Illustrations and Photographs by the Author. Crown 8vo., 6*s*.

Lees and Clutterbuck.—B.C. 1887: *A Ramble in British Columbia.* By J. A. Lees and W. J. Clutterbuck. With Map and 75 Illustrations. Crown 8vo., 3*s*. 6*d*.

Macdonald.—*The Gold Coast: Past and Present.* By George Macdonald, Director of Education and H.M. Inspector of Schools for the Gold Coast Colony and the Protectorate. With 32 Illustrations. Crown 8vo., 7*s*. 6*d*.

Nansen.—*The First Crossing of Greenland.* By Fridtjof Nansen. With 143 Illustrations and a Map. Crown 8vo., 3*s*. 6*d*.

Travel and Adventure, the Colonies, &c.—*continued.*

Rice. *Occasional Essays on Native South Indian Life.* By Stanley P. Rice, Indian Civil Service. 8vo.

Smith.—*Climbing in the British Isles* By W. P. Haskett Smith. With Illustrations by Ellis Carr, and Numerous Plans.

Part I. *England.* 16mo., 3*s.* 6*d.*

Part II. *Wales and Ireland.* 16mo., 3*s.* 6*d.*

Stephen.—*The Play-Ground of Europe* (The Alps). By Leslie Stephen. With 4 Illustrations. Crown 8vo., 3*s.* 6*d.*

Three in Norway. By Two of Them. With a Map and 59 Illustrations. Crown 8vo., 2*s.* boards, 2*s.* 6*d.* cloth.

Tyndall.—(John).

The Glaciers of the Alps: being a Narrative of Excursions and Ascents. An Account of the Origin and Phenomena of Glaciers, and an Exposition of the Physical Principles to which they are related. With 61 Illustrations. Crown 8vo., 6*s.* 6*d.* net.

Hours of Exercise in the Alps. With 7 Illustrations. Cr. 8vo., 6*s.* 6*d.* net.

Sport and Pastime.

THE BADMINTON LIBRARY.

Edited by HIS GRACE THE LATE DUKE OF BEAUFORT, K.G., and A. E. T. WATSON. Complete in 29 Volumes. Crown 8vo., Cloth, Price 10*s.* 6*d.* each Volume.

*** *The Volumes are also issued half-bound in Leather, with gilt top. The price can be had from all Booksellers.*

ARCHERY. By C. J. Longman and Col. H. Walrond. With Contributions by Miss Legh, Viscount Dillon, etc. With 2 Maps, 23 Plates and 172 Illustrations in the Text. Crown 8vo., 10*s.* 6*d.*

ATHLETICS. By Montague Shearman. With Chapters on Athletics at School by W. Beacher Thomas; Athletic Sports in America by C. H. Sherrill; a Contribution on Paper-chasing by W. Rye, and an Introduction by Sir Richard Webster, Q.C., M.P. With 12 Plates and 37 Illustrations in the Text. Cr. 8vo., 10*s.* 6*d.*

BIG GAME SHOOTING. By Clive Phillipps-Wolley.

Vol. I. AFRICA AND AMERICA. With Contributions by Sir Samuel W. Baker, W. C. Oswell, F. C. Selous, etc. With 20 Plates and 57 Illustrations in the Text. Crown 8vo., 10*s.* 6*d.*

Vol. II. EUROPE, ASIA, AND THE ARCTIC REGIONS. With Contributions by Lieut.-Colonel R. Heber Percy, Major Algernon C. Heber Percy, etc. With 17 Plates and 56 Illustrations in the Text. Cr. 8vo., 10*s.* 6*d.*

BILLIARDS. By Major W. Broadfoot, R.E. With Contributions by A. H. Boyd, Sydenham Dixon, W. J. Ford, etc. With 11 Plates, 19 Illustrations in the Text, and numerous Diagrams. Cr. 8vo., 10*s.* 6*d.*

COURSING AND FALCONRY. By Harding Cox, Charles Richardson, and the Hon. Gerald Lascelles. With 20 Plates and 55 Illustrations in the Text. Crown 8vo., 10*s.* 6*d.*

CRICKET. By A. G. Steel and the Hon. R. H. Lyttelton. With Contributions by Andrew Lang, W. G. Grace, F. Gale, etc. With 13 Plates and 52 Illustrations in the Text. Crown 8vo., 10*s.* 6*d.*

CYCLING. By the Earl of Albemarle and G. Lacy Hillier. With 19 Plates and 44 Illustrations in the Text. Crown 8vo., 10*s.* 6*d.*

Sport and Pastime—*continued.*

THE BADMINTON LIBRARY—*continued.*

DANCING. By Mrs. LILLY GROVE, F.R.G.S. With Contributions by Miss MIDDLETON, The Hon. Mrs. ARMYTAGE, etc. With Musical Examples, and 38 Full-page Plates and 93 Illustrations in the Text. Crown 8vo., 10*s*. 6*d*.

DRIVING. By His Grace the late DUKE OF BEAUFORT, K.G. With Contributions by A. E. T. WATSON the EARL OF ONSLOW, etc. With 12 Plates and 54 Illustrations in the Text. Crown 8vo., 10*s*. 6*d*.

FENCING, BOXING, AND WRESTLING. By WALTER H. POLLOCK, F. C. GROVE, C. PREVOST, E. B. MITCHELL, and WALTER ARMSTRONG. With 18 Plates and 24 Illust. in the Text. Cr. 8vo., 10*s*. 6*d*.

FISHING. By H. CHOLMONDELEY-PENNELL

Vol. I. SALMON AND TROUT. With Contributions by H. R. FRANCIS, Major JOHN P. TRAHERNE, etc. With 9 Plates and numerous Illustrations of Tackle, etc. Crown 8vo., 10*s*. 6*d*.

Vol. II. PIKE AND OTHER COARSE FISH. With Contributions by the MARQUIS OF EXETER, WILLIAM SENIOR, G. CHRISTOPHER DAVIS, etc. With 7 Plates and numerous Illustrations of Tackle, etc. Crown 8vo., 10*s*. 6*d*.

FOOTBALL. By MONTAGUE SHEARMAN, W. J. OAKLEY, G. O. SMITH, FRANK MITCHELL, etc. With 19 Plates and 35 Illustrations in the Text. Cr. 8vo., 10*s*. 6*d*.

GOLF. By HORACE G. HUTCHINSON. With Contributions by the Rt. Hon. A. J. BALFOUR, M.P., Sir WALTER SIMPSON, Bart., ANDREW LANG, etc. With 32 Plates and 57 Illustrations in the Text. Cr. 8vo., 10*s*. 6*d*.

HUNTING. By His Grace the late DUKE OF BEAUFORT, K.G., and MOWBRAY MORRIS. With Contributions by the EARL OF SUFFOLK AND BERKSHIRE, Rev. E. W. L. DAVIES, G. H. LONGMAN, etc. With 5 Plates and 54 Illustrations in the Text. Crown 8vo., 10*s*. 6*d*.

MOUNTAINEERING. By C. T. DENT. With Contributions by the Right Hon. J. BRYCE, M.P., Sir MARTIN CONWAY, D. W. FRESHFIELD, C. E. MATTHEWS, etc. With 13 Plates and 91 Illustrations in the Text. Crown 8vo., 10*s*. 6*d*.

POETRY OF SPORT (THE).—Selected by HEDLEY PEEK. With a Chapter on Classical Allusions to Sport by ANDREW LANG, and a Special Preface to the BADMINTON LIBRARY by A. E. T. WATSON. With 32 Plates and 74 Illustrations in the Text. Crown 8vo., 10*s*. 6*d*.

RACING AND STEEPLE-CHASING. By the EARL OF SUFFOLK AND BERKSHIRE, W. G. CRAVEN, the Hon. F. LAWLEY, ARTHUR COVENTRY, and A. E. T. WATSON. With Frontispiece and 56 Illustrations in the Text. Crown 8vo., 10*s*. 6*d*.

RIDING AND POLO. By Captain ROBERT WEIR, J. MORAY BROWN, T. F. DALE, THE LATE DUKE OF BEAUFORT, THE EARL OF SUFFOLK AND BERKSHIRE, etc. With 18 Plates and 41 Illustrations in the Text. Crown 8vo., 10*s*. 6*d*.

ROWING. By R. P. P. ROWE and C. M. PITMAN. With Chapters on Steering by C. P. SEROCOLD and F. C. BEGG; Metropolitan Rowing by S. LE BLANC SMITH; and on PUNTING by P. W. SQUIRE. With 75 Illustrations. Crown 8vo., 10*s*. 6*d*.

SEA FISHING. By JOHN BICKERDYKE, Sir H. W. GORE-BOOTH, ALFRED C. HARMSWORTH, and W. SENIOR. With 22 Full-page Plates and 175 Illustrations in the Text. Crown 8vo., 10*s*. 6*d*.

SHOOTING.

Vol. I. FIELD AND COVERT. By LORD WALSINGHAM and Sir RALPH PAYNE-GALLWEY, Bart. With Contributions by the Hon. GERALD LASCELLES and A. J. STUART-WORTLEY. With 11 Plates and 95 Illusts. in the Text. Cr. 8vo., 10*s*. 6*d*.

Vol. II. MOOR AND MARSH. By LORD WALSINGHAM and Sir RALPH PAYNE-GALLWEY, Bart. With Contributions by LORD LOVAT and Lord CHARLES LENNOX KERR. With 8 Plates and 57 Illustrations in the Text. Crown 8vo., 10*s*. 6*d*.

Sport and Pastime—*continued.*

THE BADMINTON LIBRARY—*continued.*

SKATING, CURLING, TOBOGGANING. By J. M. HEATHCOTE, C. G. TEBBUTT, T. MAXWELL WITHAM, Rev. JOHN KERR, ORMOND HAKE, HENRY A. BUCK, etc. With 12 Plates and 272 Illustrations in the Text. Crown 8vo., 10s. 6*d.*

SWIMMING. By ARCHIBALD SINCLAIR and WILLIAM HENRY, Hon. Secs. of the Life-Saving Society. With 13 Plates and 112 Illustrations in the Text. Cr. 8vo., 10s. 6*d.*

TENNIS, LAWN TENNIS, RACKETS AND FIVES. By J. M. and C. G. HEATHCOTE, E. O. PLEYDELL-BOUVERIE, and A. C. AINGER. With Contributions by the Hon. A. LYTTELTON, W. C. MARSHALL, Miss L. DOD, etc. With 12 Plates and 67 Illustrations in the Text. Cr. 8vo., 10s. 6*d.*

YACHTING.

Vol. I. CRUISING, CONSTRUCTION OF YACHTS, YACHT RACING RULES, FITTING-OUT, etc. By Sir EDWARD SULLIVAN, Bart., THE EARL OF PEMBROKE, LORD BRASSEY, K.C.B., C. E. SETH-SMITH, C.B., G. L. WATSON, R. T. PRITCHETT, E. F. KNIGHT, etc. With 21 Plates and 93 Illustrations in the Text. Crown 8vo., 10s. 6*d.*

Vol. II. YACHT CLUBS, YACHTING IN AMERICA AND THE COLONIES, YACHT RACING, etc By R. T. PRITCHETT, THE MARQUIS OF DUFFERIN AND AVA, K.P., THE EARL OF ONSLOW, JAMES MCFERRAN, etc. With 35 Plates and 160 Illustrations in the Text. Crown 8vo., 10s. 6*d.*

FUR, FEATHER, AND FIN SERIES.

Edited by A. E. T. WATSON.

Crown 8vo., price 5*s.* each Volume, cloth.

*** *The Volumes are also issued half-bound in Leather, with gilt top. The price can be had from all Booksellers.*

THE PARTRIDGE. Natural History, by the Rev. H. A. MACPHERSON; Shooting, by A. J. STUART-WORTLEY; Cookery, by GEORGE SAINTSBURY. With 11 Illustrations and various Diagrams in the Text. Crown 8vo., 5*s.*

THE GROUSE. Natural History, by the Rev. H. A. MACPHERSON; Shooting, by A. J. STUART-WORTLEY; Cookery, by GEORGE SAINTSBURY. With 13 Illustrations and various Diagrams in the Text. Crown 8vo., 5*s.*

THE PHEASANT. Natural History, by the Rev. H. A. MACPHERSON; Shooting, by A. J. STUART-WORTLEY: Cookery, by ALEXANDER INNES SHAND. With 10 Illustrations and various Diagrams. Crown 8vo., 5*s.*

THE HARE. Natural History, by the Rev. H. A. MACPHERSON; Shooting, by the Hon. GERALD LASCELLES; Coursing, by CHARLES RICHARDSON: Hunting, by J. S. GIBBONS and G. H. LONGMAN; Cookery, by Col. KENNEY HERBERT. With 9 Illustrations. Crown 8vo, 5*s.*

RED DEER.—Natural History, by the Rev. H. A. MACPHERSON; Deer Stalking, by CAMERON OF LOCHIEL; Stag Hunting, by Viscount EBRINGTON; Cookery, by ALEXANDER INNES SHAND. With 10 Illustrations. Crown 8vo., 5*s.*

THE SALMON. By the Hon. A. E. GATHORNE-HARDY. With Chapters on the Law of Salmon Fishing by CLAUD DOUGLAS PENNANT; Cookery, by ALEXANDER INNES SHAND. With 8 Illustrations. Cr. 8vo., 5*s.*

THE TROUT. By the MARQUESS OF GRANBY. With Chapters on the Breeding of Trout by Col. H. CUSTANCE; and Cookery, by ALEXANDER INNES SHAND. With 12 Illustrations. Crown 8vo., 5*s.*

THE RABBIT. By JAMES EDMUND HARTING. Cookery, by ALEXANDER INNES SHAND. With 10 Illustrations. Cr. 8vo., 5*s.*

PIKE AND PERCH. By WILLIAM SENIOR ('Redspinner,' Editor of the 'Field'). With Chapters by JOHN BICKERDYKE and W. H. POPE; Cookery, by ALEXANDER INNES SHAND. With 12 Illustrations. Crown 8vo., 5*s.*

Sport and Pastime—*continued.*

Bickerdyke.—*DAYS OF MY LIFE ON WATERS FRESH AND SALT, AND OTHER PAPERS.* By JOHN BICKERDYKE. With Photo-etching Frontispiece and 8 Full-page Illustrations. Crown 8vo., 6*s*.

Blackburne. — *MR. BLACKBURNE'S GAMES AT CHESS.* Selected, Annotated and Arranged by Himself. Edited, with a Biographical Sketch and a brief History of Blindfold Chess, by P. ANDERSON GRAHAM. 8vo., 7*s*. 6*d*. net.

Cawthorne and Herod.—*ROYAL ASCOT:* its History and its Associations. By GEORGE JAMES CAWTHORNE and RICHARD S. HEROD. With 32 Plates and 106 Illustrations in the Text. Demy 4to., 31*s*. 6*d*. net.

Chess Congress, 1899. The Book of the London International. Royal 8vo. 15*s*. net.

Chess Tournament for Masters and Amateurs. A Memorial of an Invitation. Arranged by, and Played at, the City of London Chess Club, 7 Grocers' Hall Court, Poultry, E.C., in April and May, 1900. Containing the Full Scores of the Games Played. 8vo., 2*s*.

Dead Shot (The): or, Sportsman's Complete Guide. Being a Treatise on the Use of the Gun, with Rudimentary and Finishing Lessons in the Art of Shooting Game of all kinds. Also Game-driving, Wildfowl and Pigeon-shooting, Dog-breaking, etc. By MARKSMAN. With numerous Illustrations. Crown 8vo., 10*s*. 6*d*.

Ellis.—*CHESS SPARKS;* or, Short and Bright Games of Chess. Collected and Arranged by J. H. ELLIS, M.A. 8vo., 4*s*. 6*d*.

Folkard.—*THE WILD-FOWLER:* A Treatise on Fowling, Ancient and Modern, descriptive also of Decoys and Flight-ponds, Wild-fowl Shooting, Gunning-punts, Shooting-yachts, etc. Also Fowling in the Fens and in Foreign Countries, Rock-fowling, etc., etc., by H. C. FOLKARD. With 13 Engravings on Steel, and several Woodcuts. 8vo., 12*s*. 6*d*.

Ford.—*THE THEORY AND PRACTICE OF ARCHERY.* By HORACE FORD. New Edition, thoroughly Revised and Re-written by W. BUTT, M.A. With a Preface by C. J. LONGMAN, M.A. 8vo., 14*s*.

Ford.—*MIDDLESEX COUNTY CRICKET CLUB,* 1864-1899. Written and Compiled by W. J. FORD. With Photogravure Portrait of V. E. Walker. 8vo., 10*s*. net.

Francis.—*A BOOK ON ANGLING:* or, Treatise on the Art of Fishing in every Branch; including full Illustrated List of Salmon Flies. By FRANCIS FRANCIS. With Portrait and Coloured Plates. Crown 8vo., 15*s*.

Gibson.—*TOBOGGANING ON CROOKED RUNS.* By the Hon. HARRY GIBSON. With Contributions by F. DE B. STRICKLAND and 'LADY-TOBOGANNER'. With 40 Illustrations. Crown 8vo., 6*s*.

Graham.—*COUNTRY PASTIMES FOR BOYS.* By P. ANDERSON GRAHAM. With 252 Illustrations from Drawings and Photographs. Crown 8vo., 3*s*. 6*d*.

Hardy.—*AUTUMNS IN ARGYLESHIRE WITH ROD AND GUN.* By the Hon. A. GATHORNE-HARDY. With 8 Photogravure Illustrations from Original Drawings by ARCHIBALD THORBURN. 8vo., 10*s*. 6*d*. net.

Hutchinson.—*THE BOOK OF GOLF AND GOLFERS.* By HORACE G. HUTCHINSON. With Contributions by Miss AMY PASCOE, H. H. HILTON, J. H. TAYLOR, H. J. WHIGHAM, and Messrs. SUTTON & SONS. With 71 Portraits, etc. Large crown 8vo., 7*s*. 6*d*. net.

Lang.—*ANGLING SKETCHES.* By ANDREW LANG. With 20 Illustrations. Crown 8vo., 3*s*. 6*d*.

Lillie (ARTHUR).

CROQUET: its History, Rules and Secrets. With 4 Full-page Illustrations by LUCIEN DAVIS, 15 Illustrations in the Text, and 27 Diagrams. Crown 8vo., 6*s*.

CROQUET UP TO DATE. Containing the Ideas and Teachings of the Leading Players and Champions. With 19 Illustrations (15 Portraits), and numerous Diagrams. 8vo., 10*s*. 6*d*. net.

Longman.—*CHESS OPENINGS.* By FREDERICK W. LONGMAN. Fcp. 8vo., 2*s*. 6*d*.

Madden.—*THE DIARY OF MASTER WILLIAM SILENCE:* a Study of Shakespeare and of Elizabethan Sport. By the Right Hon. D. H. MADDEN, Vice-Chancellor of the University of Dublin. 8vo., 16*s*.

Maskelyne.—*SHARPS AND FLATS:* a Complete Revelation of the Secrets of Cheating at Games of Chance and Skill. By JOHN NEVIL MASKELYNE, of the Egyptian Hall. With 62 Illustrations. Crown 8vo., 6*s*.

Moffat.—*CRICKETY CRICKET:* Rhymes and Parodies. By DOUGLAS MOFFAT, with Frontispiece by the late Sir FRANK LOCKWOOD, and 53 Illustrations by the Author. Crown 8vo, 2*s*. 6*d*.

Sport and Pastime—*continued.*

Park. *The Game of Golf.* By William Park, Jun., Champion Golfer, 1887-89. With 17 Plates and 26 Illustrations in the Text. Crown 8vo., 7s. 6d.

Payne-Gallwey (Sir Ralph, Bart.).

Letters to Young Shooters (First Series). On the Choice and use of a Gun With 41 Illustrations. Crown 8vo., 7s. 6d.

Letters to Young Shooters (Second Series). On the Production, Preservation, and Killing of Game. With Directions in Shooting Wood-Pigeons and Breaking-in Retrievers. With Portrait and 103 Illustrations. Crown 8vo., 12s. 6d.

Letters to Young Shooters. (Third Series.) Comprising a Short Natural History of the Wildfowl that are Rare or Common to the British Islands, with complete directions in Shooting Wildfowl on the Coast and Inland. With 200 Illustrations. Crown 8vo., 18s.

Pole—*The Theory of the Modern Scientific Game of Whist.* By William Pole, F.R.S. Fcp. 8vo., 2s. 6d.

Proctor.—*How to Play Whist: with the Laws and Etiquette of Whist.* By Richard A. Proctor. Crown 8vo., 3s. 6d.

Ribblesdale.—*The Queen's Hounds and Stag-Hunting Recollections.* By Lord Ribblesdale, Master of the Buckhounds, 1892-95. With Introductory Chapter on the Hereditary Mastership by E. Burrows. With 24 Plates and 35 Illustrations in the Text. 8vo., 25s.

Ronalds.—*The Fly-Fisher's Entomology.* By Alfred Ronalds. With 20 coloured Plates. 8vo., 14s.

Selous.—*Sport and Travel, East and West.* By Frederick Courteney Selous. With 18 Plates and 35 Illustrations in the Text. Medium 8vo., 12s. 6d. net.

Wilcocks.—*The Sea Fisherman:* Comprising the Chief Methods of Hook and Line Fishing in the British and other Seas, and Remarks on Nets, Boats, and Boating. By J. C. Wilcocks. Illustrated. Cr. 8vo., 6s.

Mental, Moral, and Political Philosophy.

LOGIC, RHETORIC, PSYCHOLOGY, &C.

Abbott.—*The Elements of Logic.* By T. K. Abbott, B.D. 12mo., 3s.

Aristotle.

The Ethics: Greek Text, Illustrated with Essay and Notes. By Sir Alexander Grant, Bart. 2 vols. 8vo., 32s.

An Introduction to Aristotle's Ethics. Books I.-IV. (Book X. c. vi.-ix. in an Appendix). With a continuous Analysis and Notes. By the Rev. E. Moore, D.D. Crown 8vo. 10s. 6d.

Bacon (Francis).

Complete Works. Edited by R. L. Ellis, James Spedding and D. D. Heath. 7 vols. 8vo., £3 13s. 6d.

Letters and Life, including all his occasional Works. Edited by James Spedding. 7 vols. 8vo., £4 4s.

The Essays: with Annotations. By Richard Whately, D.D. 8vo., 10s. 6d.

The Essays: with Notes. By F. Storr and C. H. Gibson. Cr. 8vo, 3s. 6d.

The Essays: with Introduction, Notes, and Index. By E. A. Abbott, D.D. 2 Vols. Fcp. 8vo., 6s. The Text and Index only, without Introduction and Notes, in One Volume. Fcp. 8vo., 2s. 6d.

Bain (Alexander).

Mental and Moral Science: a Compendium of Psychology and Ethics. Crown 8vo., 10s. 6d.

Or separately,

Part I. *Psychology and History of Philosophy.* Crown 8vo., 6s. 6d.

Part II. *Theory of Ethics and Ethical Systems.* Crown 8vo., 4s. 6d.

Senses and the Intellect. 8vo., 15s.

Emotions and the Will. 8vo., 15s.

Logic. Part I. *Deduction.* Crown 8vo., 4s. Part II. *Induction.* Crown 8vo., 6s. 6d.

Practical Essays. Cr. 8vo., 2s.

Bray.—*The Philosophy of Necessity:* or, Law in Mind as in Matter. By Charles Bray. Crown 8vo., 5s.

Crozier (John Beattie).

Civilisation and Progress: being the Outlines of a New System of Political, Religious and Social Philosophy. 8vo., 14s.

History of Intellectual Development: on the Lines of Modern Evolution.

Vol. I. Greek and Hindoo Thought; Græco-Roman Paganism; Judaism; and Christianity down to the Closing of the Schools of Athens by Justinian, 529 A.D. 8vo., 14s.

Mental, Moral and Political Philosophy—*continued.*

LOGIC, RHETORIC, PSYCHOLOGY, &c.

Davidson.—*The Logic of Definition*, Explained and Applied. By William L. Davidson, M.A. Crown 8vo., 6s.

Green (Thomas Hill).—The Works of. Edited by R. L. Nettleship.

Vols. I. and II. Philosophical Works. 8vo., 16s. each.

Vol. III. Miscellanies. With Index to the three Volumes, and Memoir. 8vo., 21s.

Lectures on the Principles of Political Obligation. With Preface by Bernard Bosanquet. 8vo., 5s.

Gurnhill.—*The Morals of Suicide.* By the Rev. J. Gurnhill, B.A. Crown 8vo., 6s.

Hodgson (Shadworth H.)

Time and Space: A Metaphysical Essay. 8vo., 16s.

The Theory of Practice: an Ethical Inquiry. 2 vols. 8vo., 24s.

The Philosophy of Reflection. 2 vols. 8vo., 21s.

The Metaphysic of Experience. Book I. General Analysis of Experience; Book II. Positive Science; Book III. Analysis of Conscious Action; Book IV. The Real Universe. 4 vols. 8vo., 36s. net.

Hume.—*The Philosophical Works of David Hume.* Edited by T. H. Green and T. H. Grose. 4 vols. 8vo., 28s. Or separately, Essays. 2 vols. 14s. Treatise of Human Nature. 2 vols. 14s.

James.—*The Will to Believe*, and Other Essays in Popular Philosophy. By William James, M.D., LL.D., etc. Crown 8vo., 7s. 6d.

Justinian.—*The Institutes of Justinian:* Latin Text, chiefly that of Huschke, with English Introduction, Translation, Notes, and Summary. By Thomas C. Sandars, M.A. 8vo., 18s.

Kant (Immanuel).

Critique of Practical Reason, and Other Works on the Theory of Ethics. Translated by T. K. Abbott, B.D. With Memoir. 8vo., 12s. 6d.

Fundamental Principles of the Metaphysic of Ethics. Translated by T. K. Abbott, B.D. Crown 8vo, 3s.

Introduction to Logic, and his Essay on the Mistaken Subtilty of the Four Figures. Translated by T. K. Abbott. 8vo., 6s.

Kelly.—*Government or Human Evolution.—Justice.* By Edmond Kelly, M.A., F.G.S. Cr. 8vo., 7s. 6d. net.

Killick.—*Handbook to Mill's System of Logic.* By Rev. A. H. Killick, M.A. Crown 8vo., 3s. 6d.

Ladd (George Trumbull).

A Theory of Reality: an Essay in Metaphysical System upon the Basis of Human Cognitive Experience. 8vo., 18s.

Elements of Physiological Psychology. 8vo., 21s.

Outlines of Descriptive Psychology: a Text-Book of Mental Science for Colleges and Normal Schools. 8vo., 12s.

Outlines of Physiological Psychology. 8vo., 12s.

Primer of Psychology. Cr. 8vo., 5s. 6d.

Lecky.—*The Map of Life:* Conduct and Character. By William Edward Hartpole Lecky. 8vo., 10s. 6d.

Lutoslawski.—*The Origin and Growth of Plato's Logic.* With an Account of Plato's Style and of the Chronology of his Writings. By Wincenty Lutoslawski. 8vo., 21s.

Max Müller (F.).

The Science of Thought. 8vo., 21s.

The Six Systems of Indian Philosophy. 8vo., 18s.

Mill (John Stuart).

A System of Logic. Cr. 8vo., 3s. 6d.

On Liberty. Crown 8vo., 1s. 4d.

Considerations on Representative Government. Crown 8vo., 2s.

Utilitarianism. 8vo., 2s. 6d.

Examination of Sir William Hamilton's Philosophy. 8vo., 16s.

Nature, the Utility of Religion, and Theism. Three Essays. 8vo., 5s.

Monck.—*An Introduction to Logic.* By William Henry S. Monck, M.A. Crown 8vo., 5s.

Romanes.—*Mind and Motion and Monism.* By George John Romanes, LL.D., F.R.S. Cr. 8vo., 4s. 6d.

Stock.—*Lectures in the Lyceum;* or, Aristotle's Ethics for English Readers. Edited by St. George Stock. Crown 8vo., 7s. 6d.

Mental, Moral, and Political Philosophy—*continued.*

Sully (JAMES).

THE HUMAN MIND: a Text-book of Psychology. 2 vols. 8vo., 21s.

OUTLINES OF PSYCHOLOGY. Crown 8vo., 9s.

THE TEACHER'S HANDBOOK OF PSYCHOLOGY. Crown 8vo., 6s. 6d.

STUDIES OF CHILDHOOD. 8vo., 10s. 6d.

CHILDREN'S WAYS: being Selections from the Author's 'Studies of Childhood'. With 25 Illustrations. Crown 8vo., 4s. 6d.

Sutherland.—*THE ORIGIN AND GROWTH OF THE MORAL INSTINCT.* By ALEXANDER SUTHERLAND, M.A. 2 vols. 8vo, 28s.

Swinburne.—*PICTURE LOGIC:* an Attempt to Popularise the Science of Reasoning. By ALFRED JAMES SWINBURNE, M.A. With 23 Woodcuts. Cr. 8vo., 2s. 6d.

Webb.—*THE VEIL OF ISIS:* a Series of Essays on Idealism. By THOMAS E. WEBB, LL.D., Q.C. 8vo., 10s. 6d.

Weber.—*HISTORY OF PHILOSOPHY.* By ALFRED WEBER, Professor in the University of Strasburg. Translated by FRANK THILLY, Ph.D. 8vo., 16s.

Whately (ARCHBISHOP).

BACON'S ESSAYS. With Annotations. 8vo., 10s. 6d.

ELEMENTS OF LOGIC. Cr. 8vo., 4s. 6d.

ELEMENTS OF RHETORIC. Cr. 8vo., 4s. 6d.

Zeller (Dr. EDWARD).

THE STOICS, EPICUREANS, AND SCEPTICS. Translated by the Rev. O. J. REICHEL, M.A. Crown 8vo., 15s.

OUTLINES OF THE HISTORY OF GREEK PHILOSOPHY. Translated by SARAH F. ALLEYNE and EVELYN ABBOTT, M.A., LL.D. Crown 8vo., 10s. 6d.

PLATO AND THE OLDER ACADEMY. Translated by SARAH F. ALLEYNE and ALFRED GOODWIN, B.A. Crown 8vo., 18s.

SOCRATES AND THE SOCRATIC SCHOOLS. Translated by the Rev. O. J. REICHEL, M.A. Crown 8vo., 10s. 6d.

ARISTOTLE AND THE EARLIER PERIPATETICS. Translated by B. F. C. COSTELLOE, M.A., and J. H. MUIRHEAD, M.A. 2 vols. Crown 8vo., 24s.

STONYHURST PHILOSOPHICAL SERIES.

A MANUAL OF POLITICAL ECONOMY. By C. S. DEVAS, M.A. Crown 8vo., 6s. 6d.

FIRST PRINCIPLES OF KNOWLEDGE. By JOHN RICKABY, S.J. Crown 8vo., 5s.

GENERAL METAPHYSICS. By JOHN RICKABY, S.J. Crown 8vo., 5s.

LOGIC. By RICHARD F. CLARKE, S.J. Crown 8vo., 5s.

MORAL PHILOSOPHY (ETHICS AND NATURAL LAW). By JOSEPH RICKABY, S.J. Crown 8vo., 5s.

NATURAL THEOLOGY. By BERNARD BOEDDER, S.J. Crown 8vo., 6s. 6d.

PSYCHOLOGY. By MICHAEL MAHER, S.J. Crown 8vo., 6s. 6d.

History and Science of Language, &c.

Davidson.—*LEADING AND IMPORTANT ENGLISH WORDS:* Explained and Exemplified. By WILLIAM L. DAVIDSON, M.A. Fcp. 8vo., 3s. 6d.

Farrar.—*LANGUAGE AND LANGUAGES.* By F. W. FARRAR, D.D., Dean of Canterbury. Crown 8vo., 6s.

Graham.—*ENGLISH SYNONYMS,* Classified and Explained: with Practical Exercises. By G. F. GRAHAM. Fcp. 8vo., 6s.

Max Muller (F.).

THE SCIENCE OF LANGUAGE.—Founded on Lectures delivered at the Royal Institution in 1861 and 1863. 2 vols. Crown 8vo., 10s.

BIOGRAPHIES OF WORDS, AND THE HOME OF THE ARYAS. Crown 8vo., 5s.

Roget.—*THESAURUS OF ENGLISH WORDS AND PHRASES.* Classified and Arranged so as to Facilitate the Expression of Ideas and assist in Literary Composition. By PETER MARK ROGET, M.D., F.R.S. With full Index. Crown 8vo., 10s. 6d.

Whately.—*ENGLISH SYNONYMS.* By E. JANE WHATELY. Fcp. 8vo., 3s.

Political Economy and Economics.

Ashley.—*English Economic History and Theory.* By W. J. Ashley, M.A. Cr. 8vo., Part I., 5s. Part II., 10s. 6d.

Bagehot.—*Economic Studies.* By Walter Bagehot. Crown 8vo., 3s. 6d.

Barnett.—*Practicable Socialism:* Essays on Social Reform. By Samuel A. and Henrietta Barnett. Crown 8vo., 6s.

Devas.—*A Manual of Political Economy.* By C. S. Devas, M.A. Cr. 8vo., 6s. 6d. (*Stonyhurst Philosophical Series.*)

Jordan.—*The Standard of Value.* By William Leighton Jordan. Cr. 8vo., 6s.

Leslie.—*Essays on Political Economy.* By T. E. Cliffe Leslie, Hon. LL.D., Dubl. 8vo., 10s. 6d.

Macleod (Henry Dunning).

Bimetalism. 8vo., 5s. net.

The Elements of Banking. Cr. 8vo., 3s. 6d.

The Theory and Practice of Banking. Vol. I. 8vo., 12s. Vol. II. 14s.

The Theory of Credit. 8vo. In 1 Vol., 30s. net; or separately, Vol. I., 10s. net. Vol. II., Part I., 10s. net. Vol II., Part II. 10s. net.

Mill.—*Political Economy.* By John Stuart Mill.

Popular Edition. Crown 8vo., 3s. 6d.
Library Edition. 2 vols. 8vo., 30s.

Mulhall.—*Industries and Wealth of Nations.* By Michael G. Mulhall, F.S.S. With 32 Diagrams. Cr. 8vo., 8s. 6d.

Spahr. — *America's Working People.* By Charles B. Spahr. Crown 8vo., 5s. net.

Symes.—*Political Economy.* With a Supplementary Chapter on Socialism. By J. E. Symes, M.A. Crown 8vo., 2s. 6d.

Toynbee.—*Lectures on the Industrial Revolution of the 18th Century in England.* By Arnold Toynbee. With a Memoir of the Author by Benjamin Jowett, D.D. 8vo., 10s. 6d.

Webb (Sidney and Beatrice).

The History of Trade Unionism. With Map and full Bibliography of the Subject. 8vo., 18s.

Industrial Democracy: a Study in Trade Unionism. 2 vols. 8vo., 25s. net.

Problems of Modern Industry: Essays. 8vo., 7s. 6d.

Wright.—*Outline of Practical Sociology.* With Special Reference to American Conditions. By Carroll D. Wright, LL.D. With 12 Maps and Diagrams. Crown 8vo., 9s.

Evolution, Anthropology, &c.

Clodd (Edward).

The Story of Creation: a Plain Account of Evolution. With 77 Illustrations. Crown 8vo., 3s. 6d.

A Primer of Evolution: being a Popular Abridged Edition of 'The Story of Creation'. With Illustrations. Fcp. 8vo., 1s. 6d.

Lang (Andrew).

Custom and Myth: Studies of Early Usage and Belief. With 15 Illustrations. Crown 8vo., 3s. 6d.

Myth, Ritual, and Religion. 2 vols. Crown 8vo., 7s.

Modern Mythology: a Reply to Professor Max Müller. 8vo., 9s.

Lubbock.—*The Origin of Civilisation,* and the Primitive Condition of Man. By Sir J. Lubbock, Bart., M.P. (Lord Avebury). With 5 Plates and 20 Illustrations. 8vo., 18s.

Romanes (George John).

Darwin, and after Darwin: an Exposition of the Darwinian Theory, and a Discussion on Post-Darwinian Questions.

Part I. The Darwinian Theory. With Portrait of Darwin and 125 Illustrations. Crown 8vo., 10s. 6d.

Part II. Post-Darwinian Questions: Heredity and Utility. With Portrait of the Author and 5 Illustrations. Cr. 8vo., 10s. 6d.

Part III. Post-Darwinian Questions: Isolation and Physiological Selection. Crown 8vo., 5s.

An Examination of Weismannism. Crown 8vo., 6s.

Essays. Edited by C. Lloyd Morgan, Principal of University College, Bristol. Crown 8vo., 6s.

Classical Literature, Translations, &c.

Abbott.—*Hellenica.* A Collection of Essays on Greek Poetry, Philosophy, History, and Religion. Edited by Evelyn Abbott, M.A., LL.D. Crown 8vo., 7s. 6d.

Æschylus.—*Eumenides of Æschylus.* With Metrical English Translation. By J. F. Davies. 8vo., 7s.

Aristophanes.—*The Acharnians of Aristophanes*, translated into English Verse. By R. Y. Tyrrell. Crown 8vo., 1s.

Becker (W. A.), Translated by the Rev. F. Metcalfe, B.D.

Gallus: or, Roman Scenes in the Time of Augustus. With Notes and Excursuses. With 26 Illustrations. Crown 8vo., 3s. 6d.

Charicles: or, Illustrations of the Private Life of the Ancient Greeks. With Notes and Excursuses. With 26 Illustrations. Crown 8vo., 3s. 6d.

Butler.—*The Authoress of the Odyssey, where and when She wrote, who She was, the Use She made of the Iliad, and how the Poem grew under Her hands.* By Samuel Butler. With 14 Illustrations and 4 Maps. 8vo., 10s. 6d.

Campbell.—*Religion in Greek Literature.* By the Rev. Lewis Campbell, M.A., LL.D. 8vo., 15s.

Cicero.—*Cicero's Correspondence.* By R. Y. Tyrrell. Vols. I., II., III., 8vo., each 12s. Vol. IV., 15s. Vol. V., 14s. Vol. VI., 12s.

Harvard Studies in Classical Philology, 1900. Edited by a Committee of the Classical Instructors of Harvard University. Vol. XI. 8vo., 6s. 6d. net.

Hime.—*Lucian, the Syrian Satirist.* By Lieut.-Col. Henry W. L. Hime, (late) Royal Artillery. 8vo., 5s. net.

Homer.

The Iliad of Homer. Freely rendered into English Prose for the use of those who cannot read the original. By Samuel Butler, Author of 'Erewhon,' etc. Crown 8vo., 7s. 6d.

The Odyssey of Homer. Freely rendered into English Prose for the use of those that cannot read the original. By Samuel Butler. 8vo., 7s. 6d.

The Odyssey of Homer. Done into English Verse. By William Morris. Crown 8vo., 6s.

Horace.—*The Works of Horace, rendered into English Prose.* With Life, Introduction and Notes. By William Coutts, M.A. Crown 8vo., 5s. net.

Lang.—*Homer and the Epic.* By Andrew Lang. Crown 8vo., 9s. net.

Lucan.—*The Pharsalia of Lucan.* Translated into Blank Verse. By Sir Edward Ridley. 8vo., 14s.

Mackail.—*Select Epigrams from the Greek Anthology.* By J. W. Mackail. Edited with a Revised Text, Introduction, Translation, and Notes. 8vo., 16s.

Rich.—*A Dictionary of Roman and Greek Antiquities.* By A. Rich, B.A. With 2000 Woodcuts. Crown 8vo., 6s. net.

Sophocles.—Translated into English Verse. By Robert Whitelaw, M.A., Assistant Master in Rugby School. Cr. 8vo., 8s. 6d.

Tyrrell.—*Dublin Translations into Greek and Latin Verse.* Edited by R. Y. Tyrrell. 8vo., 6s.

Virgil.

The Æneid of Virgil. Translated into English Verse by John Conington. Crown 8vo., 6s.

The Poems of Virgil. Translated into English Prose by John Conington. Crown 8vo., 6s.

The Æneids of Virgil. Done into English Verse. By William Morris. Crown 8vo., 6s.

The Æneid of Virgil, freely translated into English Blank Verse. By W. J. Thornhill. Crown 8vo., 6s. net.

The Æneid of Virgil. Translated into English Verse by James Rhoades.

Books I.-VI. Crown 8vo., 5s.

Books VII.-XII. Crown 8vo., 5s.

The Eclogues and Georgics of Virgil. Translated into English Prose by J. W. Mackail, Fellow of Balliol College, Oxford. 16mo., 5s.

Wilkins.—*The Growth of the Homeric Poems.* By G. Wilkins. 8vo., 6s.

Poetry and the Drama.

Arnold.—*The Light of the World:* or, The Great Consummation. By Sir Edwin Arnold. With 14 Illustrations after Holman Hunt. Crown 8vo., 6*s*.

Bell (Mrs. Hugh).

Chamber Comedies: a Collection of Plays and Monologues for the Drawing Room. Crown 8vo., 6*s*

Fairy Tale Plays, and How to Act Them. With 91 Diagrams and 52 Illustrations. Crown 8vo., 3*s*. 6*d*.

Coleridge.—*Selections from.* With Introduction by Andrew Lang. With 18 Illustrations by Patten Wilson. Crown 8vo., 3*s*. 6*d*.

Goethe.—*The First Part of the Tragedy of Faust in English.* By Thos. E. Webb, LL.D., sometime Fellow of Trinity College; Professor of Moral Philosophy in the University of Dublin, etc. New and Cheaper Edition, with *The Death of Faust*, from the Second Part. Crown 8vo., 6*s*.

Ingelow (Jean).

Poetical Works. Complete in One Volume. Crown 8vo., 6*s*. net.

Lyrical and other Poems. Selected from the Writings of Jean Ingelow. Fcp. 8vo., 2*s*. 6*d*. cloth plain, 3*s*. cloth gilt.

Lang (Andrew).

Grass of Parnassus. Fcp. 8vo., 2*s*. 6*d*. net.

The Blue Poetry Book. Edited by Andrew Lang. With 100 Illustrations. Crown 8vo., 6*s*.

Lecky.—*Poems.* By the Right Hon. W. E. H. Lecky. Fcp. 8vo., 5*s*.

Lytton (The Earl of), (Owen Meredith).

The Wanderer. Cr. 8vo., 10*s*. 6*d*.

Lucile. Crown 8vo., 10*s*. 6*d*.

Selected Poems. Cr. 8vo., 10*s*. 6*d*.

Macaulay.—*Lays of Ancient Rome, with 'Ivry' and 'The Armada'.* By Lord Macaulay.

Illustrated by G. Scharf. Fcp. 4to., 10*s*. 6*d*.

——— Bijou Edition. 18mo., 2*s*. 6*d*. gilt top.

——— Popular Edition. Fcp. 4to., 6*d*. sewed, 1*s*. cloth.

Illustrated by J. R. Weguelin. Crown 8vo., 3*s*. 6*d*.

Annotated Edition. Fcp. 8vo., 1*s*. sewed, 1*s*. 6*d*. cloth.

MacDonald (George, LL.D.).

A Book of Strife, in the Form of the Diary of an Old Soul: Poems. 18mo., 6*s*.

Rampolli: Growths from a Long-planted Root: being Translations, New and Old (mainly in verse), chiefly from the German; along with 'A Year's Diary of an Old Soul'. Crown 8vo., 6*s*.

Moffat.—*Crickety Cricket:* Rhymes and Parodies. By Douglas Moffat. With Frontispiece by the late Sir Frank Lockwood, and 53 Illustrations by the Author. Crown 8vo, 2*s*. 6*d*.

Moon.—*Poems of Love and Home,* etc. By George Washington Moon, Hon. F.R.S.L., Author of 'Elijah,' etc. 16mo., 2*s*. 6*d*.

Morris (William).

POETICAL WORKS—Library Edition.

The Earthly Paradise. 4 vols. Crown 8vo., 5*s*. net each.

The Life and Death of Jason. Crown 8vo., 5*s*. net.

The Defence of Guenevere, and other Poems. Crown 8vo., 5*s*. net.

The Story of Sigurd the Volsung, and The Fall of the Niblungs. Cr. 8vo., 5*s*. net.

Poems by the Way, and Love is Enough. Crown 8vo., 5*s*. net.

The Odyssey of Homer. Done into English Verse. Crown 8vo., 5*s*. net.

The Æneids of Virgil. Done into English Verse. Crown 8vo., 5*s*. net.

The Tale of Beowulf, sometime King of the Folk of the Weder-geats. Translated by William Morris and A. J. Wyatt. Crown 8vo., 5*s*. net.

Poetry and the Drama—*continued.*

Morris (WILLIAM) —*continued.*

Certain of the POETICAL WORKS may also be had in the following Editions:

THE EARTHLY PARADISE.

Popular Edition. 5 vols. 12mo., 25*s.*; or 5*s.* each, sold separately.

The same in Ten Parts, 25*s.*; or 2*s.* 6*d.* each, sold separately.

Cheap Edition, in 1 vol. Crown 8vo., 6*s.* net.

POEMS BY THE WAY. Square crown 8vo., 6*s.*

⁂ For Mr. William Morris's Prose Works, see pp. 22 and 31.

Morte Arthur: an Alliterative Poem of the Fourteenth Century. Edited from the Thornton MS., with Introduction, Notes and Glossary. By MARY MACLEOD BANKS. Fcp. 8vo., 3*s.* 6*d.*

Nesbit.—*LAYS AND LEGENDS.* By E. NESBIT (Mrs. HUBERT BLAND). First Series. Crown 8vo., 3*s.* 6*d.* Second Series. With Portrait. Crown 8vo., 5*s.*

Pooler.—*TRANSLATIONS*, and other Verses. By C. K. POOLER, M.A. Fcp. 8vo., 3*s.* net.

Riley.—*OLD FASHIONED ROSES:* Poems. By JAMES WHITCOMB RILEY. 12mo., 5*s.*

Romanes.—*A SELECTION FROM THE POEMS OF GEORGE JOHN ROMANES, M.A., LL.D., F.R.S.* With an Introduction by T. HERBERT WARREN, President of Magdalen College, Oxford. Crown 8vo., 4*s.* 6*d.*

Shakespeare.

BOWDLER'S FAMILY SHAKESPEARE. With 36 Woodcuts. 1 vol. 8vo., 14*s.* Or in 6 vols. Fcp. 8vo., 21*s.*

SHAKESPEARE'S SONNETS. Reconsidered, and in part Rearranged, with Introductory Chapters and a Reprint of the Original 1609 Edition, by SAMUEL BUTLER, Author of 'Erewhon'. 8vo., 10*s.* 6*d.*

THE SHAKESPEARE BIRTHDAY BOOK. By MARY F. DUNBAR. 32mo., 1*s.* 6*d.*

Wagner.—*THE NIBELUNGEN RING.* Done into English Verse by REGINALD RANKIN, B.A. of the Inner Temple, Barrister-at-Law. Vol. I. Rhine Gold and Valkyrie. Fcp. 8vo., 4*s.* 6*d.*

Wordsworth.—*SELECTED POEMS.* By ANDREW LANG. With Photogravure Frontispiece of Rydal Mount. With 16 Illustrations and numerous Initial Letters. By ALFRED PARSONS, A.R.A. Crown 8vo., gilt edges, 3*s.* 6*d.*

Fiction, Humour, &c.

Anstey.—*VOCES POPULI.* Reprinted from 'Punch'. By F. ANSTEY, Author of 'Vice Versâ'. First Series. With 20 Illustrations by J. BERNARD PARTRIDGE. Crown 8vo., 3*s.* 6*d.*

Beaconsfield (THE EARL OF).

NOVELS AND TALES. Complete in 11 vols. Crown 8vo., 1*s.* 6*d.* each.

Vivian Grey.	Sybil.
The Young Duke, etc.	Henrietta Temple.
Alroy, Ixion, etc.	Venetia.
Contarini Fleming, etc.	Coningsby.
	Lothair.
Tancred.	Endymion.

NOVELS AND TALES. THE HUGHENDEN EDITION. With 2 Portraits and 11 Vignettes. 11 Vols. Crown 8vo., 42*s.*

Birt.—*CASTLE CZVARGAS:* a Romance. Being a Plain Story of the Romantic Adventures of Two Brothers, Told by the Younger of Them. Edited by ARCHIBALD BIRT. Crown 8vo., 6*s.*

Churchill.—*SAVROLA:* a Tale of the Revolution in Laurania. By WINSTON SPENCER CHURCHILL, M.P. Cr. 8vo., 6*s.*

Dougall.—*BEGGARS ALL.* By L. DOUGALL. Crown 8vo., 3*s.* 6*d.*

Fiction, Humour, &c.—*continued.*

Doyle (A. Conan).

Micah Clarke: A Tale of Monmouth's Rebellion. With 10 Illustrations. Cr. 8vo., 3s. 6d.

The Captain of the Polestar, and other Tales. Cr. 8vo., 3s. 6d.

The Refugees: A Tale of the Huguenots. With 25 Illustrations. Cr. 8vo., 3s. 6d.

The Stark Munro Letters. Cr. 8vo, 3s. 6d.

Farrar (F. W., Dean of Canterbury).

Darkness and Dawn: or, Scenes in the Days of Nero. An Historic Tale. Cr. 8vo., 6s. net.

Gathering Clouds: a Tale of the Days of St. Chrysostom. Cr. 8vo., 6s. net.

Fowler (Edith H.).

The Young Pretenders. A Story of Child Life. With 12 Illustrations by Sir Philip Burne-Jones, Bart. Crown 8vo., 6s.

The Professor's Children. With 24 Illustrations by Ethel Kate Burgess. Crown 8vo., 6s.

Francis.—*Yeoman Fleetwood*. By M. E. Francis, Author of 'In a North-country Village,' etc. Crown 8vo., 6s.

Froude.—*The Two Chiefs of Dunboy*: an Irish Romance of the Last Century. By James A. Froude. Cr. 8vo., 3s. 6d.

Haggard (H. Rider).

Black Heart and White Heart, and other Stories. With 33 Illustrations. Crown 8vo., 6s.

Swallow: a Tale of the Great Trek. With 8 Illustrations. Crown 8vo., 6s.

Dr. Therne. Crown 8vo., 3s. 6d.

Heart of the World. With 15 Illustrations. Crown 8vo., 3s. 6d.

Haggard (H. Rider)—*continued.*

Joan Haste. With 20 Illustrations. Crown 8vo., 3s. 6d.

The People of the Mist. With 16 Illustrations. Crown 8vo., 3s. 6d.

Montezuma's Daughter. With 24 Illustrations. Crown 8vo., 3s. 6d.

She. With 32 Illustrations. Crown 8vo., 3s. 6d.

Allan Quatermain. With 31 Illustrations. Crown 8vo., 3s. 6d.

Maiwa's Revenge. Cr. 8vo., 1s. 6d.

Colonel Quaritch, V.C. With Frontispiece and Vignette. Cr. 8vo., 3s. 6d.

Cleopatra. With 29 Illustrations. Crown 8vo., 3s. 6d.

Beatrice. With Frontispiece and Vignette. Cr. 8vo., 3s. 6d.

Eric Brighteyes. With 51 Illustrations. Crown 8vo., 3s. 6d.

Nada the Lily. With 23 Illustrations. Crown 8vo., 3s. 6d.

Allan's Wife. With 34 Illustrations. Crown 8vo., 3s. 6d.

The Witch's Head. With 16 Illustrations. Crown 8vo., 3s. 6d.

Mr. Meeson's Will. With 16 Illustrations. Crown 8vo., 3s. 6d.

Dawn. With 16 Illustrations. Cr. 8vo., 3s. 6d.

Haggard and Lang.—*The World's Desire*. By H. Rider Haggard and Andrew Lang. With 27 Illustrations. Crown 8vo., 3s. 6d.

Harte.—*In the Carquinez Woods*. By Bret Harte. Crown 8vo., 3s. 6d.

Hope.—*The Heart of Princess Osra*. By Anthony Hope. With 9 Illustrations. Crown 8vo., 3s. 6d.

Fiction, Humour, &c.—*continued.*

Jerome. *SKETCHES IN LAVENDER: BLUE AND GREEN.* By JEROME K. JEROME. Crown 8vo., 3s. 6d.

Joyce.—*OLD CELTIC ROMANCES.* Twelve of the most beautiful of the Ancient Irish Romantic Tales. Translated from the Gaelic. By P. W. JOYCE, LL.D. Crown 8vo., 3s. 6d.

Lang.—*A MONK OF FIFE*; a Story of the Days of Joan of Arc. By ANDREW LANG. With 13 Illustrations by SELWYN IMAGE. Crown 8vo., 3s. 6d.

Levett-Yeats. — *THE CHEVALIER D'AURIAC.* By S. LEVETT-YEATS. Crown 8vo., 3s. 6d.

Lyall (EDNA).

THE AUTOBIOGRAPHY OF A SLANDER. Fcp. 8vo., 1s., sewed.
Presentation Edition. With 20 Illustrations by LANCELOT SPEED. Crown 8vo., 2s. 6d. net.

THE AUTOBIOGRAPHY OF A TRUTH. Fcp. 8vo., 1s., sewed; 1s. 6d., cloth.

DOREEN. The Story of a Singer. Crown 8vo., 6s.

WAYFARING MEN. Crown 8vo., 6s.

HOPE THE HERMIT: a Romance of Borrowdale. Crown 8vo., 6s.

Mason and Lang.—*PARSON KELLY.* By A. E. W. MASON and ANDREW LANG. Crown 8vo., 6s.

Max Müller. — *DEUTSCHE LIEBE (GERMAN LOVE)*: Fragments from the Papers of an Alien. Collected by F. MAX MÜLLER. Translated from the German by G. A. M. Crown 8vo., 5s.

Melville (G. J. WHYTE).

The Gladiators.	Holmby House.
The Interpreter.	Kate Coventry.
Good for Nothing.	Digby Grand.
The Queen's Maries.	General Bounce.

Crown 8vo., 1s. 6d. each.

Merriman.—*FLOTSAM*: A Story of the Indian Mutiny. By HENRY SETON MERRIMAN. Crown 8vo., 3s. 6d.

Morris (WILLIAM).

THE SUNDERING FLOOD. Cr. 8vo., 7s. 6d.

THE WATER OF THE WONDROUS ISLES. Crown 8vo., 7s. 6d.

THE WELL AT THE WORLD'S END. 2 vols. 8vo., 28s.

THE STORY OF THE GLITTERING PLAIN, which has been also called The Land of the Living Men, or The Acre of the Undying. Square post 8vo., 5s. net.

THE ROOTS OF THE MOUNTAINS, wherein is told somewhat of the Lives of the Men of Burgdale, their Friends, their Neighbours, their Foemen, and their Fellows-in-Arms. Written in Prose and Verse. Square crown 8vo., 8s.

A TALE OF THE HOUSE OF THE WOLFINGS, and all the Kindreds of the Mark. Written in Prose and Verse. Square crown 8vo., 6s.

A DREAM OF JOHN BALL, AND A KING'S LESSON. 12mo., 1s. 6d.

NEWS FROM NOWHERE; or, An Epoch of Rest. Being some Chapters from an Utopian Romance. Post 8vo., 1s. 6d.

THE STORY OF GRETTIR THE STRONG. Translated from the Icelandic by EIRÍKR MAGNÚSSON and WILLIAM MORRIS. Cr. 8vo., 5s. net.

*** For Mr. William Morris's Poetical Works, see p. 19.

Newman (CARDINAL).

LOSS AND GAIN: The Story of a Convert. Crown 8vo. Cabinet Edition, 6s.; Popular Edition, 3s. 6d.

CALLISTA: A Tale of the Third Century. Crown 8vo. Cabinet Edition, 6s.; Popular Edition, 3s. 6d.

Phillipps-Wolley.—*SNAP*: a Legend of the Lone Mountain. By C. PHILLIPPS-WOLLEY. With 13 Illustrations. Crown 8vo., 3s. 6d.

Raymond (WALTER).

TWO MEN O' MENDIP. Cr. 8vo., 6s.

NO SOUL ABOVE MONEY. Cr. 8vo., 6s.

Fiction, Humour, &c.—*continued.*

Reader.—*Priestess and Queen*: a Tale of the White Race of Mexico; being the Adventures of Ignigene and her Twenty-six Fair Maidens. By Emily E. Reader. Illustrated by Emily K. Reader. Crown 8vo., 6*s.*

Sewell (Elizabeth M.).

A Glimpse of the World.	Amy Herbert.
Laneton Parsonage.	Cleve Hall.
Margaret Percival.	Gertrude.
Katharine Ashton.	Home Life.
The Earl's Daughter.	After Life.
The Experience of Life.	Ursula. Ivors.

Cr. 8vo., 1*s.* 6*d.* each cloth plain. 2*s.* 6*d.* each cloth extra, gilt edges.

Somerville and Ross.—*Some Experiences of an Irish R.M.* By E. Œ. Somerville and Martin Ross. With 31 Illustrations by E. Œ. Somerville. Crown 8vo., 6*s.*

Stebbing.—*Probable Tales.* Edited by William Stebbing. Crown 8vo., 4*s.* 6*d.*

Stevenson (Robert Louis).

The Strange Case of Dr. Jekyll and Mr. Hyde. Fcp. 8vo., 1*s.* sewed. 1*s.* 6*d.* cloth.

The Strange Case of Dr. Jekyll and Mr. Hyde; with other Fables. Crown 8vo., 3*s.* 6*d.*

More New Arabian Nights—The Dynamiter. By Robert Louis Stevenson and Fanny van de Grift Stevenson. Crown 8vo., 3*s.* 6*d.*

The Wrong Box. By Robert Louis Stevenson and Lloyd Osbourne. Crown 8vo., 3*s.* 6*d.*

Suttner.—*Lay Down Your Arms* (*Die Waffen Nieder*): The Autobiography of Martha von Tilling. By Bertha von Suttner. Translated by T. Holmes. Cr. 8vo., 1*s.* 6*d.*

Taylor.—*Early Italian Love-Stories.* Taken from the Originals by Una Taylor. With 13 Illustrations by Henry J. Ford. Crown 4to., 15*s.* net.

Trollope (Anthony).

The Warden. Cr. 8vo., 1*s.* 6*d.*

Barchester Towers. Cr. 8vo., 1*s.* 6*d.*

Walford (L. B.).

Mr. Smith: a Part of his Life. Crown 8vo., 2*s.* 6*d.*

The Baby's Grandmother. Cr. 8vo., 2*s.* 6*d.*

Cousins. Crown 8vo., 2*s.* 6*d.*

Troublesome Daughters. Cr. 8vo., 2*s.* 6*d.*

Pauline. Crown 8vo., 2*s.* 6*d.*

Dick Netherby. Cr. 8vo., 2*s.* 6*d.*

The History of a Week. Cr. 8vo. 2*s.* 6*d.*

A Stiff-necked Generation. Cr. 8vo. 2*s.* 6*d.*

Nan, and other Stories. Cr. 8vo., 2*s.* 6*d.*

The Mischief of Monica. Cr. 8vo., 2*s.* 6*d.*

The One Good Guest. Cr. 8vo. 2*s.* 6*d.*

'*Ploughed*,' and other Stories. Crown 8vo., 2*s.* 6*d.*

The Matchmaker. Cr. 8vo., 2*s.* 6*d.*

The Intruders. Crown 8vo., 2*s.* 6*d.*

Leddy Marget. Crown 8vo., 2*s.* 6*d.*

Iva Kildare: a Matrimonial Problem. Crown 8vo., 2*s.* 6*d.*

Ward.—*One Poor Scruple.* By Mrs. Wilfrid Ward. Crown 8vo., 6*s.*

West.—*Edmund Fulleston*; or, The Family Evil Genius. By B. B. West, Author of 'Half Hours with the Millionaires,' etc. Crown 8vo., 6*s.*

Weyman (Stanley).

Sophia. With Frontispiece. Crown 8vo., 6*s.*

The House of the Wolf. With Frontispiece and Vignette. Crown 8vo., 3*s.* 6*d.*

A Gentleman of France. With Frontispiece and Vignette. Cr. 8vo., 6*s.*

The Red Cockade. With Frontispiece and Vignette. Crown 8vo., 6*s.*

Shrewsbury. With 24 Illustrations by Claude A. Shepperson. Cr. 8vo., 6*s.*

Popular Science (Natural History, &c.).

Beddard.—*The Structure and Classification of Birds.* By Frank E. Beddard, M.A., F.R.S., Prosector and Vice-Secretary of the Zoological Society of London. With 252 Illustrations. 8vo., 21s. net.

Butler.—*Our Household Insects.* An Account of the Insect-Pests found in Dwelling-Houses. By Edward A. Butler, B.A., B.Sc. (Lond.). With 113 Illustrations. Crown 8vo., 3s. 6d.

Furneaux (W.).

The Outdoor World; or The Young Collector's Handbook. With 18 Plates (16 of which are coloured), and 549 Illustrations in the Text. Crown 8vo., 6s. net.

Butterflies and Moths (British). With 12 coloured Plates and 241 Illustrations in the Text. Crown 8vo., 6s. net.

Life in Ponds and Streams. With 8 coloured Plates and 331 Illustrations in the Text. Crown 8vo., 6s. net.

Hartwig (George).

The Sea and its Living Wonders. With 12 Plates and 303 Woodcuts. 8vo., 7s. net.

The Tropical World. With 8 Plates and 172 Woodcuts. 8vo., 7s. net.

The Polar World. With 3 Maps, 8 Plates and 85 Woodcuts. 8vo., 7s. net.

The Subterranean World. With 3 Maps and 80 Woodcuts. 8vo., 7s. net.

Heroes of the Polar World. With 19 Illustrations. Cr. 8vo., 2s.

Wonders of the Tropical Forests. With 40 Illustrations. Cr. 8vo., 2s.

Workers under the Ground. With 29 Illustrations. Cr. 8vo., 2s.

Marvels Over our Heads. With 29 Illustrations. Cr. 8vo., 2s.

Sea Monsters and Sea Birds. With 75 Illustrations. Cr. 8vo., 2s. 6d.

Denizens of the Deep. With 117 Illustrations. Cr. 8vo., 2s. 6d.

Hartwig (George)—*continued.*

Volcanoes and Earthquakes. With 30 Illustrations. Cr. 8vo., 2s. 6d.

Wild Animals of the Tropics. With 66 Illustrations. Cr. 8vo., 3s. 6d.

Helmholtz.—*Popular Lectures on Scientific Subjects.* By Hermann von Helmholtz. With 68 Woodcuts. 2 vols. Cr. 8vo., 3s. 6d. each.

Hudson (W. H.).

Nature in Downland. With 12 Plates and 14 Illustrations in the Text by A. D. McCormick. 8vo., 10s. 6d. net.

British Birds. With a Chapter on Structure and Classification by Frank E. Beddard, F.R.S. With 16 Plates (8 of which are Coloured), and over 100 Illustrations in the Text. Cr. 8vo., 6s. net.

Birds in London. With 17 Plates and 15 Illustrations in the Text, by Bryan Hook, A. D. McCormick, and from Photographs from Nature, by R. B. Lodge. 8vo., 12s.

Proctor (Richard A.).

Light Science for Leisure Hours. Familiar Essays on Scientific Subjects. Vol. I. Crown 8vo., 3s. 6d.

Rough Ways made Smooth. Familiar Essays on Scientific Subjects. Crown 8vo., 3s. 6d.

Pleasant Ways in Science. Crown 8vo., 3s. 6d.

Nature Studies. By R. A. Proctor, Grant Allen, A. Wilson, T. Foster and E. Clodd. Crown 8vo., 3s. 6d.

Leisure Readings. By R. A. Proctor, E. Clodd, A. Wilson, T. Foster and A. C. Ranyard. Cr. 8vo., 3s. 6d.

*** *For Mr. Proctor's other books see pp. 14 and 28, and Messrs. Longmans & Co.'s Catalogue of Scientific Works.*

Stanley.—*A Familiar History of Birds.* By E. Stanley, D.D., formerly Bishop of Norwich. With 160 Illustrations. Cr. 8vo., 3s. 6d.

Popular Science (Natural History, &c.)—*continued.*

Wood (Rev. J. G.).

Homes without Hands: A Description of the Habitations of Animals, classed according to the Principle of Construction. With 140 Illustrations. 8vo., 7s. net.

Insects at Home: A Popular Account of British Insects, their Structure, Habits and Transformations. With 700 Illustrations. 8vo., 7s. net.

Out of Doors; a Selection of Original Articles on Practical Natural History. With 11 Illustrations. Cr. 8vo., 3s. 6d.

Strange Dwellings: a Description of the Habitations of Animals, abridged from 'Homes without Hands'. With 60 Illustrations. Cr. 8vo., 3s. 6d.

Wood (Rev. J. G.)—*continued.*

Petland Revisited. With 33 Illustrations. Cr. 8vo., 3s. 6d.

Bird Life of the Bible. With 32 Illustrations. Cr. 8vo., 3s. 6d.

Wonderful Nests. With 30 Illustrations. Cr. 8vo., 3s. 6d.

Homes under the Ground. With 28 Illustrations. Cr. 8vo., 3s. 6d.

Wild Animals of the Bible. With 29 Illustrations. Cr. 8vo., 3s. 6d.

Domestic Animals of the Bible. With 23 Illustrations. Cr. 8vo., 3s. 6d.

The Branch Builders. With 28 Illustrations. Cr. 8vo., 2s. 6d.

Social Habitations and Parasitic Nests. With 18 Illustrations. Cr. 8vo., 2s.

Works of Reference.

Gwilt.—*An Encyclopædia of Architecture.* By Joseph Gwilt, F.S.A. With 1700 Engravings. Revised (1888), with Alterations and Considerable Additions by Wyatt Papworth. 8vo., 21s. net.

Maunder (Samuel).

Biographical Treasury. With Supplement brought down to 1889. By Rev. James Wood. Fcp. 8vo., 6s.

Treasury of Geography, Physical, Historical, Descriptive, and Political. With 7 Maps and 16 Plates. Fcp. 8vo., 6s.

The Treasury of Bible Knowledge. By the Rev. J. Ayre, M.A. With 5 Maps, 15 Plates, and 300 Woodcuts. Fcp. 8vo., 6s.

Treasury of Knowledge and Library of Reference. Fcp. 8vo., 6s.

Historical Treasury. Fcp. 8vo., 6s.

Maunder (Samuel)—*continued.*

The Treasury of Botany. Edited by J. Lindley, F.R.S., and T. Moore, F.L.S. With 274 Woodcuts and 20 Steel Plates. 2 vols. Fcp. 8vo., 12s.

Roget. — *Thesaurus of English Words and Phrases.* Classified and Arranged so as to Facilitate the Expression of Ideas and assist in Literary Composition. By Peter Mark Roget, M.D., F.R.S. Recomposed throughout, enlarged and improved, partly from the Author's Notes, and with a full Index, by the Author's Son, John Lewis Roget. Crown 8vo., 10s. 6d.

Willich.—*Popular Tables* for giving information for ascertaining the value of Lifehold, Leasehold, and Church Property, the Public Funds, etc. By Charles M. Willich. Edited by H. Bence Jones. Crown 8vo., 10s. 6d.

Children's Books.

Buckland.—*Two Little Runaways.* Adapted from the French of Louis Desnoyers. By James Buckland. With 110 Illustrations by Cecil Aldin. Cr. 8vo., 6s.

Corbin and Going.—*Urchins of the Sea.* By Marie Overton Corbin and Charles Buxton Going. With Drawings by F. I. Bennett. Oblong 4to., 3s. 6d.

Crake (Rev. A. D.).

Edwy the Fair; or, The First Chronicle of Æscendune. Cr. 8vo., 2s. 6d.

Crake (Rev. A. D.)—*continued.*

Alfgar the Dane; or, The Second Chronicle of Æscendune. Cr. 8vo. 2s. 6d.

The Rival Heirs: being the Third and Last Chronicle of Æscendune. Cr. 8vo., 2s. 6d.

The House of Walderne. A Tale of the Cloister and the Forest in the Days of the Barons' Wars. Crown 8vo., 2s. 6d.

Brian Fitz-Count. A Story of Wallingford Castle and Dorchester Abbey. Cr. 8vo., 2s. 6d.

Children's Books—*continued*.

Henty (G. A.). EDITED BY.

YULE LOGS: A Story-Book for Boys. By VARIOUS AUTHORS. With 61 Illustrations. Crown 8vo., 6s.

YULE TIDE YARNS: a Story-Book for Boys. By VARIOUS AUTHORS. With 45 Illustrations. Crown 8vo., 6s.

Lang (ANDREW).—EDITED BY.

THE BLUE FAIRY BOOK. With 138 Illustrations. Crown 8vo., 6s.

THE RED FAIRY BOOK. With 100 Illustrations. Crown 8vo., 6s.

THE GREEN FAIRY BOOK. With 99 Illustrations. Crown 8vo., 6s.

THE YELLOW FAIRY BOOK. With 104 Illustrations. Crown 8vo., 6s.

THE PINK FAIRY BOOK. With 67 Illustrations. Crown 8vo., 6s.

THE GREY FAIRY BOOK. With 65 Illustrations. Crown 8vo., 6s.

THE BLUE POETRY BOOK. With 100 Illustrations. Crown 8vo., 6s.

THE BLUE POETRY BOOK. School Edition, without Illustrations. Fcp. 8vo., 2s. 6d.

THE TRUE STORY BOOK. With 66 Illustrations. Crown 8vo., 6s.

THE RED TRUE STORY BOOK. With 100 Illustrations. Crown 8vo., 6s.

THE ANIMAL STORY BOOK. With 67 Illustrations. Crown 8vo., 6s.

THE RED BOOK OF ANIMAL STORIES. With 65 Illustrations. Crown 8vo., 6s.

THE ARABIAN NIGHTS ENTERTAINMENTS. With 66 Illustrations. Cr. 8vo., 6s.

Meade (L. T.).

DADDY'S BOY. With 8 Illustrations. Crown 8vo., 3s. 6d.

DEB AND THE DUCHESS. With 7 Illustrations. Crown 8vo., 3s. 6d.

THE BERESFORD PRIZE. With 7 Illustrations. Crown 8vo., 3s. 6d.

THE HOUSE OF SURPRISES. With 6 Illustrations. Crown 8vo. 3s. 6d.

Praeger (ROSAMOND).

THE ADVENTURES OF THE THREE BOLD BABES: HECTOR, HONORIA AND ALISANDER. A Story in Pictures. With 24 Coloured Plates and 24 Outline Pictures. Oblong 4to., 3s. 6d.

THE FURTHER DOINGS OF THE THREE BOLD BABIES. With 24 Coloured Pictures and 24 Outline Pictures. Oblong 4to., 3s. 6d.

Stevenson.—*A CHILD'S GARDEN OF VERSES.* By ROBERT LOUIS STEVENSON. Fcp. 8vo., 5s.

Upton (FLORENCE K. AND BERTHA).

THE ADVENTURES OF TWO DUTCH DOLLS AND A 'GOLLIWOGG'. With 31 Coloured Plates and numerous Illustrations in the Text. Oblong 4to., 6s.

THE GOLLIWOGG'S BICYCLE CLUB. With 31 Coloured Plates and numerous Illustrations in the Text. Oblong 4to., 6s.

THE GOLLIWOGG AT THE SEASIDE. With 31 Coloured Plates and numerous Illustrations in the Text. Oblong 4to., 6s.

THE GOLLIWOGG IN WAR. With 31 Coloured Plates. Oblong 4to., 6s.

THE GOLLIWOGG'S POLAR ADVENTURES. With 31 Coloured Plates. Oblong 4to., 6s.

THE VEGE-MEN'S REVENGE. With 31 Coloured Plates and numerous Illustrations in the Text. Oblong 4to., 6s.

The Silver Library.

CROWN 8VO. 3s. 6d. EACH VOLUME.

Arnold's (Sir Edwin) Seas and Lands. With 71 Illustrations. 3s. 6d.

Bagehot's (W.) Biographical Studies. 3s. 6d.

Bagehot's (W.) Economic Studies. 3s. 6d.

Bagehot's (W.) Literary Studies. With Portrait. 3 vols, 3s. 6d. each.

Baker's (Sir S. W.) Eight Years in Ceylon. With 6 Illustrations. 3s. 6d.

Baker's (Sir S. W.) Rifle and Hound in Ceylon. With 6 Illustrations. 3s. 6d.

Baring-Gould's (Rev. S.) Curious Myths of the Middle Ages. 3s. 6d.

Baring-Gould's (Rev. S.) Origin and Development of Religious Belief. 2 vols. 3s. 6d. each.

Becker's (W. A.) Gallus: or, Roman Scenes in the Time of Augustus. With 26 Illus., 3s. 6d.

The Silver Library—*continued.*

Becker's (W. A.) Charicles: or, Illustrations of the Private Life of the Ancient Greeks. With 26 Illustrations. 3*s.* 6*d.*

Bent's (J. T.) The Ruined Cities of Mashonaland. With 117 Illustrations. 3*s.* 6*d.*

Brassey's (Lady) A Voyage in the 'Sunbeam'. With 66 Illustrations. 3*s.* 6*d.*

Churchill's (W. S.) The Story of the Malakand Field Force, 1897. With 6 Maps and Plans. 3*s.* 6*d.*

Clodd's (E.) Story of Creation: a Plain Account of Evolution. With 77 Illustrations. 3*s.* 6*d.*

Conybeare (Rev. W. J.) and Howson's (Very Rev. J. S.) Life and Epistles of St. Paul. With 46 Illustrations. 3*s.* 6*d.*

Dougall's (L.) Beggars All: a Novel. 3*s.* 6*d.*

Doyle's (A. Conan) Micah Clarke. A Tale of Monmouth's Rebellion. With 10 Illusts. 3*s.* 6*d.*

Doyle's (A. Conan) The Captain of the Polestar, and other Tales. 3*s.* 6*d.*

Doyle's (A. Conan) The Refugees: A Tale of the Huguenots. With 25 Illustrations. 3*s* 6*d.*

Doyle's (A. Conan) The Stark Munro Letters. 3*s.* 6*d.*

Froude's (J. A.) The History of England, from the Fall of Wolsey to the Defeat of the Spanish Armada. 12 vols. 3*s.* 6*d.* each.

Froude's (J. A.) The English in Ireland. 3 vols. 10*s.* 6*d.*

Froude's (J. A.) The Divorce of Catherine of Aragon. 3*s.* 6*d.*

Froude's (J. A.) The Spanish Story of the Armada, and other Essays. 3*s.* 6*d.*

Froude's (J. A.) Short Studies on Great Subjects. 4 vols. 3*s.* 6*d.* each.

Froude's (J. A.) Oceana, or England and Her Colonies. With 9 Illustrations. 3*s.* 6*d.*

Froude's (J. A.) The Council of Trent. 3*s.* 6*d.*

Froude's (J. A.) The Life and Letters of Erasmus. 3*s.* 6*d.*

Froude's (J. A.) Thomas Carlyle: a History of his Life.
1795-1835. 2 vols. 7*s.* 1834-1881. 2 vols. 7*s.*

Froude's (J. A.) Cæsar: a Sketch. 3*s.* 6*d.*

Froude's (J. A.) The Two Chiefs of Dunboy: an Irish Romance of the Last Century. 3*s.* 6*d.*

Gleig's (Rev. G. R.) Life of the Duke of Wellington. With Portrait. 3*s.* 6*d.*

Greville's (C. C. F.) Journal of the Reigns of King George IV., King William IV., and Queen Victoria. 8 vols., 3*s.* 6*d.* each.

Haggard's (H. R.) She: A History of Adventure. With 32 Illustrations. 3*s.* 6*d.*

Haggard's (H. R.) Allan Quatermain With 20 Illustrations. 3*s.* 6*d.*

Haggard's (H. R.) Colonel Quaritch, V.C.: a Tale of Country Life. With Frontispiece and Vignette. 3*s.* 6*d.*

Haggard's (H. R.) Cleopatra. With 29 Illustrations. 3*s.* 6*d.*

Haggard's (H. R.) Eric Brighteyes. With 51 Illustrations. 3*s.* 6*d.*

Haggard's (H. R.) Beatrice. With Frontispiece and Vignette. 3*s.* 6*d.*

Haggard's (H. R.) Allan's Wife. With 34 Illustrations. 3*s.* 6*d.*

Haggard (H. R.) Heart of the World. With 15 Illustrations. 3*s.* 6*d.*

Haggard's (H. R.) Montezuma's Daughter. With 25 Illustrations. 3*s.* 6*d.*

Haggard's (H. R.) The Witch's Head. With 16 Illustrations. 3*s.* 6*d.*

Haggard's (H. R.) Mr. Meeson's Will. With 16 Illustrations. 3*s.* 6*d.*

Haggard's (H. R.) Nada the Lily. With 23 Illustrations. 3*s.* 6*d.*

Haggard's (H. R.) Dawn. With 16 Illusts. 3*s.* 6*d.*

Haggard's (H. R.) The People of the Mist. With 16 Illustrations. 3*s.* 6*d.*

Haggard's (H. R.) Joan Haste. With 20 Illustrations. 3*s.* 6*d.*

Haggard (H. R.) and Lang's (A.) The World's Desire. With 27 Illustrations. 3*s.* 6*d.*

Harte's (Bret) In the Carquinez Woods and other Stories. 3*s.* 6*d.*

Helmholtz's (Hermann von) Popular Lectures on Scientific Subjects. With 68 Illustrations. 2 vols. 3*s.* 6*d.* each.

Hope's (Anthony) The Heart of Princess Osra. With 9 Illustrations. 3*s.* 6*d.*

Hornung's (E. W.) The Unbidden Guest. 3*s.* 6*d*

Howitt's (W.) Visits to Remarkable Places. With 80 Illustrations. 3*s.* 6*d.*

Jefferies' (R.) The Story of My Heart: My Autobiography. With Portrait. 3*s.* 6*d.*

Jefferies' (R.) Field and Hedgerow. With Portrait. 3*s.* 6*d.*

Jefferies' (R.) Red Deer. With 17 Illusts. 3*s.* 6*d.*

Jefferies' (R.) Wood Magic: a Fable. With Frontispiece and Vignette by E. V. B. 3*s.* 6*d.*

Jefferies (R.) The Toilers of the Field. With Portrait from the Bust in Salisbury Cathedral. 3*s.* 6*d.*

Kaye (Sir J.) and Malleson's (Colonel) History of the Indian Mutiny of 1857-8. 6 vols. 3*s.* 6*d.* each.

Knight's (E. F.) The Cruise of the 'Alerte': the Narrative of a Search for Treasure on the Desert Island of Trinidad. With 2 Maps and 23 Illustrations. 3*s.* 6*d.*

Knight's (E. F.) Where Three Empires Meet: a Narrative of Recent Travel in Kashmir, Western Tibet, Baltistan, Gilgit. With a Map and 54 Illustrations. 3*s.* 6*d.*

The Silver Library—*continued.*

Knight's (E. F.) The 'Falcon' on the Baltic: a Coasting Voyage from Hammersmith to Copenhagen in a Three-Ton Yacht. With Map and 11 Illustrations. 3*s.* 6*d.*

Köstlin's (J.) Life of Luther. With 62 Illustrations and 4 Facsimiles of MSS. 3*s.* 6*d.*

Lang's (A.) Angling Sketches. With 20 Illustrations. 3*s.* 6*d.*

Lang's (A.) Custom and Myth: Studies of Early Usage and Belief. 3*s.* 6*d.*

Lang's (A.) Cock Lane and Common-Sense. 3*s.* 6*d.*

Lang's (A.) The Book of Dreams and Ghosts. 3*s.* 6*d.*

Lang's (A.) A Monk of Fife: a Story of the Days of Joan of Arc. With 13 Illustrations. 3*s.* 6*d.*

Lang's (A.) Myth, Ritual, and Religion. 2 vols. 7*s.*

Lees (J. A.) and Clutterbuck's (W. J.) B. C. 1887, A Ramble in British Columbia. With Maps and 75 Illustrations. 3*s.* 6*d*

Levett-Yeats' (S.) The Chevalier D'Auriac. 3*s.* 6*d.*

Macaulay's (Lord) Complete Works. 'Albany' Edition. With 12 Portraits. 12 vols. 3*s.* 6*d.* each.

Macaulay's (Lord) Essays and Lays of Ancient Rome, etc. With Portrait and 4 Illustrations to the 'Lays'. 3*s.* 6*d.*

Macleod's (H. D.) Elements of Banking. 3*s.* 6*d.*

Marbot's (Baron de) Memoirs. Translated. 2 vols. 7*s.*

Marshman's (J. C.) Memoirs of Sir Henry Havelock. 3*s.* 6*d.*

Merivale's (Dean) History of the Romans under the Empire. 8 vols. 3*s.* 6*d.* each.

Merriman's (H. S.) Flotsam: A Tale of the Indian Mutiny. 3*s.* 6*d.*

Mill's (J. S.) Political Economy. 3*s.* 6*d.*

Mill's (J. S.) System of Logic. 3*s.* 6*d.*

Milner's (Geo.) Country Pleasures: the Chronicle of a Year chiefly in a Garden. 3*s.* 6*d.*

Nansen's (F.) The First Crossing of Greenland. With 142 Illustrations and a Map. 3*s.* 6*d.*

Phillipps-Wolley's (C.) Snap: a Legend of the Lone Mountain With 13 Illustrations. 3*s.* 6*d.*

Proctor's (R. A.) The Orbs Around Us. 3*s.* 6*d.*

Proctor's (R. A.) The Expanse of Heaven. 3*s.* 6*d.*

Proctor's (R. A.) Light Science for Leisure Hours. First Series. 3*s.* 6*d.*

Proctor's (R. A.) The Moon. 3*s.* 6*d.*

Proctor's (R. A.) Other Worlds than Ours. 3*s.* 6*d.*

Proctor's (R. A.) Our Place among Infinities: a Series of Essays contrasting our Little Abode in Space and Time with the Infinities around us. 3*s.* 6*d.*

Proctor's (R. A.) Other Suns than Ours. 3*s.* 6*d.*

Proctor's (R. A.) Rough Ways made Smooth. 3*s.* 6*d.*

Proctor's (R. A.) Pleasant Ways in Science. 3*s.* 6*d.*

Proctor's (R. A.) Myths and Marvels of Astronomy. 3*s.* 6*d.*

Proctor's (R. A.) Nature Studies. 3*s.* 6*d.*

Proctor's (R. A.) Leisure Readings. By R. A. Proctor, Edward Clodd, Andrew Wilson, Thomas Foster, and A. C. Ranyard. With Illustrations. 3*s.* 6*d.*

Rossetti's (Maria F.) A Shadow of Dante. 3*s.* 6*d.*

Smith's (R. Bosworth) Carthage and the Carthaginians. With Maps, Plans, etc. 3*s.* 6*d.*

Stanley's (Bishop) Familiar History of Birds. With 160 Illustrations. 3*s.* 6*d.*

Stephen's (L.) The Playground of Europe (The Alps). With 4 Illustrations. 3*s.* 6*d.*

Stevenson's (R. L.) The Strange Case of Dr. Jekyll and Mr. Hyde; with other Fables. 3*s.* 6*d.*

Stevenson (R. L.) and Osbourne's (Ll.) The Wrong Box. 3*s.* 6*d.*

Stevenson (Robert Louis) and Stevenson's (Fanny van de Grift) More New Arabian Nights.—The Dynamiter. 3*s.* 6*d.*

Trevelyan's (Sir G. O.) The Early History of Charles James Fox. 3*s.* 6*d.*

Weyman's (Stanley J.) The House of the Wolf: a Romance. 3*s.* 6*d.*

Wood's (Rev. J. G.) Petland Revisited. With 33 Illustrations. 3*s.* 6*d.*

Wood's (Rev. J. G.) Strange Dwellings. With 60 Illustrations. 3*s.* 6*d.*

Wood's (Rev. J. G.) Out of Doors. With 11 Illustrations. 3*s.* 6*d.*

Cookery, Domestic Management, &c.

Acton. — *Modern Cookery.* By Eliza Acton. With 150 Woodcuts. Fcp. 8vo., 4*s.* 6*d.*

Ashby.—*Health in the Nursery.* By Henry Ashby, M.D., F.R.C.P., Physician to the Manchester Children's Hospital. With 25 Illustrations. Crown 8vo., 3*s.* 6*d.*

Buckton.—*Comfort and Cleanliness*: The Servant and Mistress Question. By Catherine M. Buckton. With 14 Illustrations. Crown 8vo., 2*s.*

Bull (Thomas, M.D.).

Hints to Mothers on the Management of their Health during the Period of Pregnancy. Fcp. 8vo., 1*s.* 6*d.*

The Maternal Management of Children in Health and Disease. Fcp. 8vo., 1*s.* 6*d.*

Cookery, Domestic Management, &c.—*continued.*

De Salis (Mrs.).

Cakes and Confections à la Mode. Fcp. 8vo., 1s. 6d.

Dogs: A Manual for Amateurs. Fcp. 8vo., 1s. 6d.

Dressed Game and Poultry à la Mode. Fcp. 8vo., 6d.

Dressed Vegetables à la Mode. Fcp. 8vo., 1s 6d.

Drinks à la Mode Fcp. 8vo., 1s. 6d.

Entrées à la Mode. Fcp. 8vo., 1s. 6d.

Floral Decorations. Fcp. 8vo., 1s. 6d.

Gardening à la Mode. Fcp. 8vo. Part I., Vegetables, 1s. 6d. Part II., Fruits, 1s. 6d.

National Viands à la Mode. Fcp. 8vo., 1s. 6d.

New-laid Eggs. Fcp. 8vo., 1s. 6d.

Oysters à la Mode. Fcp. 8vo., 1s. 6d.

De Salis (Mrs.).—*continued.*

Soups and Dressed Fish à la Mode. Fcp. 8vo., 1s. 6d.

Savouries à la Mode. Fcp. 8vo., 1s. 6d.

Puddings and Pastry à la Mode. Fcp. 8vo., 1s. 6d.

Sweets and Supper Dishes à la Mode. Fcp. 8vo., 1s. 6d.

Tempting Dishes for Small Incomes. Fcp. 8vo., 1s. 6d.

Wrinkles and Notions for Every Household. Crown 8vo., 1s. 6d.

Lear.—*Maigre Cookery.* By H. L. Sidney Lear. 16mo., 2s.

Mann.—*Manual of the Principles of Practical Cookery.* By E. E. Mann. Crown 8vo. 1s.

Poole.—*Cookery for the Diabetic.* By W. H. and Mrs. Poole. With Preface by Dr. Pavy. Fcp. 8vo., 2s. 6d.

Miscellaneous and Critical Works.

Bagehot.—*Literary Studies.* By Walter Bagehot. With Portrait. 3 vols. Crown 8vo., 3s. 6d. each.

Baring-Gould.—*Curious Myths of the Middle Ages.* By Rev. S. Baring-Gould. Crown 8vo., 3s. 6d.

Baynes. — *Shakespeare Studies*, and other Essays. By the late Thomas Spencer Baynes, LL.B., LL.D. With a Biographical Preface by Professor Lewis Campbell. Crown 8vo., 7s. 6d.

Boyd (A. K. H.) (**'A.K.H.B.'**).

And see Miscellaneous Theological Works, p. 32.

Autumn Holidays of a Country Parson. Crown 8vo., 3s. 6d.

Commonplace Philosopher. Cr. 8vo., 3s. 6d.

Critical Essays of a Country Parson. Crown 8vo., 3s. 6d.

East Coast Days and Memories. Crown 8vo., 3s. 6d.

Landscapes, Churches, and Moralities. Crown 8vo., 3s. 6d.

Boyd (A. K. H.) (**'A.K.H.B.'**)—*cont.*

Leisure Hours in Town. Crown 8vo., 3s. 6d.

Lessons of Middle Age. Crown 8vo., 3s. 6d.

Our Little Life. Two Series. Crown 8vo., 3s. 6d. each.

Our Homely Comedy: and Tragedy. Crown 8vo., 3s. 6d.

Recreations of a Country Parson. Three Series. Crown 8vo., 3s. 6d. each.

Burns and Colenso.—*Living Anatomy.* By Cecil L. Burns, R.B.A., and Robert J. Colenso, M.D. 40 Plates, with Descriptive Letterpress. Demy 4to. in portfolio, 7s. 6d. net.

Calder.—*Accident in Factories:* its Distribution, Causation, Compensation, and Prevention. A Practical Guide to the Law and to the Safe-Guarding, Safe Working, and Safe-Construction of Factory Machinery, Plant, and Premises. With 20 Tables and 124 Illustrations. By John Calder. Crown 8vo., 7s. 6d. net.

Miscellaneous and Critical Works—*continued.*

Charities Register, The Annual, *AND DIGEST*: being a Classified Register of Charities in or available in the Metropolis. With an Introduction by C. S. LOCH, Secretary to the Council of the Charity Organisation Society, London. 8vo., 4*s*.

Comparetti. *THE TRADITIONAL POETRY OF THE FINNS.* By DOMENICO COMPARETTI. Translated by ISABELLA M. ANDERTON. With Introduction by ANDREW LANG. 8vo., 16*s*.

Crawford.—*THE AUTOBIOGRAPHY OF A TRAMP.* By J. H. CRAWFORD. With a Photogravure Frontispiece and 8 other Illustrations. Crown 8vo., 5*s*. net.

Dickinson.—*KING ARTHUR IN CORNWALL.* By W. HOWSHIP DICKINSON, M.D. With 5 Illustrations. Crown 8vo., 4*s*. 6*d*.

Evans.—*THE ANCIENT STONE IMPLEMENTS, WEAPONS AND ORNAMENTS OF GREAT BRITAIN.* By Sir JOHN EVANS, K.C.B., D.C.L., LL.D., F.R.S., etc. With 537 Illustrations. Medium 8vo., 28*s*.

Haggard. — *A FARMER'S YEAR*: being his Commonplace Book for 1898. By H. RIDER HAGGARD. With 36 Illustrations by G. LEON LITTLE. Crown 8vo., 7*s*. 6*d*. net.

Hamlin.—*A TEXT-BOOK OF THE HISTORY OF ARCHITECTURE.* By A. D. F. HAMLIN, A.M. With 229 Illustrations. Crown 8vo., 7*s*. 6*d*.

Haweis.—*MUSIC AND MORALS.* By the Rev. H. R. HAWEIS. With Portrait of the Author, and numerous Illustrations, Facsimiles, and Diagrams. Cr. 8vo., 6*s*. net.

Hodgson.—*OUTCAST ESSAYS AND VERSE TRANSLATIONS.* By SHADWORTH H. HODGSON, LL.D. Crown 8vo., 8*s*. 6*d*.

Hoenig. — *INQUIRIES CONCERNING THE TACTICS OF THE FUTURE.* Fourth Edition, 1894, of the 'Two Brigades'. By FRITZ HOENIG. With 1 Sketch in the Text and 5 Maps. Translated by Captain H. M. BOWER. 8vo., 15*s*. net.

Hullah.—*THE HISTORY OF MODERN MUSIC.* By JOHN HULLAH. 8vo., 8*s*. 6*d*.

Jefferies (RICHARD).

FIELD AND HEDGEROW: With Portrait. Crown 8vo., 3*s*. 6*d*.

THE STORY OF MY HEART: my Autobiography. With Portrait and New Preface by C. J. LONGMAN. Cr. 8vo., 3*s*. 6*d*.

RED DEER. With 17 Illustrations. Crown 8vo., 3*s*. 6*d*.

Jefferies (RICHARD)—*continued.*

THE TOILERS OF THE FIELD. With Portrait from the Bust in Salisbury Cathedral. Crown 8vo., 3*s*. 6*d*.

WOOD MAGIC: a Fable. With Frontispiece and Vignette by E. V. B. Crown 8vo., 3*s*. 6*d*.

Jekyll (GERTRUDE).

WOOD AND GARDEN: Notes and Thoughts, Practical and Critical, of a Working Amateur. With 71 Illustrations from Photographs by the Author. 8vo., 10*s*. 6*d*. net.

HOME AND GARDEN: Notes and Thoughts, Practical and Critical, of a Worker in both. With 53 Illustrations from Photographs by the Author. 8vo., 10*s*. 6*d*. net.

Johnson (J. & J. H.).

THE PATENTEE'S MANUAL: a Treatise on the Law and Practice of Letters Patent. 8vo., 10*s*. 6*d*.

AN EPITOME OF THE LAW AND PRACTICE CONNECTED WITH PATENTS FOR INVENTIONS, with a reprint of the Patents Acts of 1883, 1885, 1886 and 1888. Crown 8vo., 2*s*. 6*d*.

Joyce.—*THE ORIGIN AND HISTORY OF IRISH NAMES OF PLACES.* By P. W. JOYCE, LL.D. 2 vols. Crown 8vo., 5*s*. each.

Kingsley.—*A HISTORY OF FRENCH ART*, 1100-1899. By ROSE G. KINGSLEY. 8vo., 12*s*. 6*d*. net.

Kristeller. — *ANDREA MANTEGNA*: his Life and Works. By PAUL KRISTELLER. English Edition by S. ARTHUR STRONG, M.A. With 25 Photogravures and 169 other Illustrations. 4to.

Lang (ANDREW).

LETTERS TO DEAD AUTHORS. Fcp. 8vo., 2*s*. 6*d*. net.

BOOKS AND BOOKMEN. With 2 Coloured Plates and 17 Illustrations. Fcp. 8vo., 2*s*. 6*d*. net.

OLD FRIENDS. Fcp. 8vo., 2*s*. 6*d*. net.

LETTERS ON LITERATURE. Fcp. 8vo., 2*s*. 6*d*. net.

ESSAYS IN LITTLE. With Portrait of the Author. Crown 8vo., 2*s*. 6*d*.

COCK LANE AND COMMON-SENSE. Crown 8vo., 3*s*. 6*d*.

THE BOOK OF DREAMS AND GHOSTS. Crown 8vo., 3*s*. 6*d*.

Miscellaneous and Critical Works—*continued.*

Macfarren. — *Lectures on Harmony.* By Sir George A. Macfarren. 8vo., 12s.

Max Müller (The Right Hon. F.).

India: What can it Teach Us? Crown 8vo., 5s.

Chips from a German Workshop.
Vol. I. Recent Essays and Addresses. Crown 8vo., 5s.
Vol. II. Biographical Essays. Crown 8vo., 5s.
Vol. III. Essays on Language and Literature. Crown 8vo., 5s.
Vol. IV. Essays on Mythology and Folk Lore. Crown 8vo., 5s.

Contributions to the Science of Mythology. 2 vols. 8vo., 32s.

Milner.—*Country Pleasures:* the Chronicle of a Year chiefly in a Garden. By George Milner. Crown 8vo., 3s. 6d.

Morris (William).

Signs of Change. Seven Lectures delivered on various Occasions. Post 8vo., 4s. 6d.

Hopes and Fears for Art. Five Lectures delivered in Birmingham, London, etc., in 1878-1881. Cr 8vo., 4s. 6d.

An Address delivered at the Distribution of Prizes to Students of the Birmingham Municipal School of Art on 21st February, 1894. 8vo., 2s. 6d. net.

Art and the Beauty of the Earth: a Lecture delivered at Burslem Town Hall, on October 13, 1881. 8vo., 2s. 6d. net.

Some Hints on Pattern-Designing: a Lecture delivered at the Working Men's College, London, on 10th December, 1881. 8vo., 2s. 6d. net.

Architecture and History, and Westminster Abbey. Two Papers read before the Society for the Protection of Ancient Buildings. 8vo., 2s. 6d. net.

Arts and Crafts Essays. By Members of the Arts and Crafts Exhibition Society. With a Preface by William Morris. Crown 8vo., 2s. 6d. net.

Pollock.—*Jane Austen:* her Contemporaries and Herself. An Essay in Criticism. By Walter Herries Pollock. Crown 8vo., 3s. 6d. net.

Poore (George Vivian, M.D., F.R.C.P.).

Essays on Rural Hygiene. With 13 Illustrations. Crown 8vo., 6s. 6d.

The Dwelling House. With 36 Illustrations. Crown 8vo., 3s. 6d.

Richter. — *Lectures on the National Gallery.* By J. P. Richter. With 20 Plates and 7 Illustrations in the Text. Crown 4to., 9s.

Rossetti.—*A Shadow of Dante:* being an Essay towards studying Himself, his World and his Pilgrimage. By Maria Francesca Rossetti. With Frontispiece by Dante Gabriel Rossetti. Crown 8vo., 3s. 6d.

Soulsby (Lucy H. M.).

Stray Thoughts on Reading. Small 8vo., 2s. 6d. net.

Stray Thoughts for Girls. 16mo., 1s. 6d. net.

Stray Thoughts for Mothers and Teachers. Small 8vo., 2s. 6d. net.

Stray Thoughts for Invalids. 16mo., 2s. net.

Stray Thoughts on Character. Small 8vo.

Southey.—*The Correspondence of Robert Southey with Caroline Bowles.* Edited, with an Introduction, by Edward Dowden, LL.D. 8vo., 14s.

Stevens.—*On the Stowage of Ships and their Cargoes.* With Information regarding Freights, Charter-Parties, etc. By Robert White Stevens, Associate-Member of the Institute of Naval Architects. 8vo., 21s.

Turner and Sutherland.—*The Development of Australian Literature.* By Henry Gyles Turner and Alexander Sutherland. With Portraits and Illustrations. Crown 8vo., 5s.

Van Dyke.—*A Text-Book on the History of Painting.* By John C. Van Dyke, Professor of the History of Art in Rutgers College, U.S. With 110 Illustrations. Crown 8vo, 6s.

Warwick.—*Progress in Women's Education in the British Empire:* being the Report of Conferences and a Congress held in connection with the Educational Section, Victorian Era Exhibition. Edited by the Countess of Warwick. Cr. 8vo. 6s.

Willard. *History of Modern Italian Art.* By Ashton Rollins Willard. With Photogravure Frontispiece and 28 Full-page Illustrations. 8vo., 18s. net.

Miscellaneous Theological Works.

*** *For Church of England and Roman Catholic Works see* MESSRS. LONGMANS & CO.'S *Special Catalogues.*

Balfour. — *THE FOUNDATIONS OF BELIEF*: being Notes Introductory to the Study of Theology. By the Right Hon. ARTHUR J. BALFOUR, M.P. 8vo., 12s. 6d.

Boyd (A. K. H.) ('**A.K.H.B.**').

COUNSEL AND COMFORT FROM A CITY PULPIT. Crown 8vo., 3s. 6d.

SUNDAY AFTERNOONS IN THE PARISH CHURCH OF A SCOTTISH UNIVERSITY CITY. Crown 8vo., 3s. 6d.

CHANGED ASPECTS OF UNCHANGED TRUTHS. Crown 8vo., 3s. 6d.

GRAVER THOUGHTS OF A COUNTRY PARSON. Three Series. Crown 8vo., 3s. 6d. each.

PRESENT DAY THOUGHTS. Crown 8vo., 3s. 6d.

SEASIDE MUSINGS. Cr. 8vo., 3s. 6d.

'*TO MEET THE DAY*' through the Christian Year: being a Text of Scripture, with an Original Meditation and a Short Selection in Verse for Every Day. Crown 8vo., 4s. 6d.

Campbell.—*RELIGION IN GREEK LITERATURE.* By the Rev. LEWIS CAMPBELL, M.A., LL.D., Emeritus Professor of Greek, University of St. Andrews. 8vo., 15s.

Davidson.—*THEISM*, as Grounded in Human Nature, Historically and Critically Handled. Being the Burnett Lectures for 1892 and 1893, delivered at Aberdeen. By W. L. DAVIDSON, M.A., LL.D. 8vo., 15s.

Gibson.—*THE ABBÉ DE LAMENNAIS AND THE LIBERAL CATHOLIC MOVEMENT IN FRANCE.* By the Hon. W. GIBSON. With Portrait. 8vo., 12s. 6d.

Lang. — *MODERN MYTHOLOGY*: a Reply to Professor Max Müller. By ANDREW LANG. 8vo., 9s.

MacDonald (GEORGE).

UNSPOKEN SERMONS. Three Series. Crown 8vo., 3s. 6d. each.

THE MIRACLES OF OUR LORD. Crown 8vo., 3s. 6d.

Martineau (JAMES).

HOURS OF THOUGHT ON SACRED THINGS: Sermons, 2 vols. Crown 8vo., 3s. 6d. each.

ENDEAVOURS AFTER THE CHRISTIAN LIFE. Discourses. Crown 8vo., 7s. 6d.

THE SEAT OF AUTHORITY IN RELIGION. 8vo., 14s.

ESSAYS, REVIEWS, AND ADDRESSES. 4 Vols. Crown 8vo., 7s. 6d. each.

HOME PRAYERS, with *TWO SERVICES* for Public Worship. Crown 8vo., 3s. 6d.

Max Müller (F.).

THE SIX SYSTEMS OF INDIAN PHILOSOPHY. 8vo., 18s.

CONTRIBUTIONS TO THE SCIENCE OF MYTHOLOGY. 2 vols. 8vo., 32s.

THE ORIGIN AND GROWTH OF RELIGION, as illustrated by the Religions of India. The Hibbert Lectures, delivered at the Chapter House, Westminster Abbey, in 1878. Crown 8vo., 5s.

INTRODUCTION TO THE SCIENCE OF RELIGION: Four Lectures delivered at the Royal Institution. Crown 8vo., 5s.

NATURAL RELIGION. The Gifford Lectures, delivered before the University of Glasgow in 1888. Crown 8vo., 5s.

PHYSICAL RELIGION. The Gifford Lectures, delivered before the University of Glasgow in 1890. Crown 8vo., 5s.

ANTHROPOLOGICAL RELIGION. The Gifford Lectures, delivered before the University of Glasgow in 1891. Cr. 8vo., 5s.

THEOSOPHY, OR PSYCHOLOGICAL RELIGION. The Gifford Lectures, delivered before the University of Glasgow in 1892. Crown 8vo., 5s.

THREE LECTURES ON THE VEDÂNTA PHILOSOPHY, delivered at the Royal Institution in March, 1894. 8vo., 5s.

RAMAKRISHNA: HIS LIFE AND SAYINGS. Crown 8vo., 5s.

Romanes.—*THOUGHTS ON RELIGION.* By GEORGE J. ROMANES, LL.D., F.R.S. Crown 8vo., 4s. 6d.

Russell.—*RELIGION AND LIFE*: a Plain Essay. By R. RUSSELL. Crown 8vo., 2s. 6d. net.

10,000/10/00.